THE REVISED VERSION
EDITED FOR THE USE OF SCHOOLS

ISAIAH
XL—LXVI

T0371046

ISAIAH
XL—LXVI

EDITED BY

THE REV. W. A. L. ELMSLIE, M.A.

AND

THE REV. JOHN SKINNER, D.D.

Cambridge:

at the University Press

1914

CAMBRIDGE
UNIVERSITY PRESS

University Printing House, Cambridge CB2 8BS, United Kingdom

Published in the United States of America by Cambridge University Press, New York

Cambridge University Press is part of the University of Cambridge.

It furthers the University's mission by disseminating knowledge in the pursuit of
education, learning and research at the highest international levels of excellence.

www.cambridge.org
Information on this title: www.cambridge.org/9781107689350

© Cambridge University Press 1914

This publication is in copyright. Subject to statutory exception
and to the provisions of relevant collective licensing agreements,
no reproduction of any part may take place without the written
permission of Cambridge University Press.

First published 1914
First paperback edition 2014

A catalogue record for this publication is available from the British Library

ISBN 978-1-107-68935-0 Paperback

Cambridge University Press has no responsibility for the persistence or accuracy of
URLs for external or third-party internet websites referred to in this publication,
and does not guarantee that any content on such websites is, or will remain, accurate
or appropriate.

PREFACE BY THE GENERAL EDITOR
FOR THE OLD TESTAMENT

THE aim of this series of commentaries is to explain the Revised Version for young students, and at the same time to present, in a simple form, the main results of the best scholarship of the day.

The General Editor has confined himself to supervision and suggestion. The writer is, in each case, responsible for the opinions expressed and for the treatment of particular passages.

A. H. M^cNEILE.

January, 1914.

CONTENTS

INTRODUCTION

IN order to understand a book of the Bible, or any other ancient document, we must know something of the circumstances under which it was written, the personality of the author, and the people for whom he was writing. Very often that information comes to us in the shape of a reliable tradition; the writing is ascribed to a certain author, and no reason is found for doubting the correctness of the ascription. But there are many cases in which, either by accident or design, a work has been attributed to an author who could not possibly have written it, or whose authorship is at least highly questionable. It is therefore essential to estimate the value of tradition in any given case and to decide whether it be sound, doubtful, or positively incredible. The method of investigation will consist chiefly in a comparison between the character and circumstances of the alleged author and the contents of the book assigned to him, the object being to determine whether such a book could have been written or could naturally be supposed to have been written by him with his known personality and his known environment.

I.

TRADITIONAL AUTHORSHIP AND EXTERNAL EVIDENCE.

The prophecies we are about to study (Is. xl.–lxvi.) are traditionally associated with the name of Isaiah, the prophet whose work has been described in the first volume of this commentary. Isaiah, the son of Amoz, was born about 770 B.C. and his prophetical activity extended from 740 B.C., the year of King Uzziah's death, to 701 B.C., when Sennacherib, King of Assyria, failed in his attempt to capture Jerusalem. In the earlier portion of the Book of Isaiah there are many prophecies which are so obviously addressed to the circumstances of that period that we cannot doubt that they are genuine utterances of this great prophet of the eighth century, although there are also strong reasons for thinking that other passages in chs. i.–xxxv. were composed by other writers at a much later time. Now the chapters before us, xl.–lxvi., also form part of the volume which is entitled the Book of Isaiah; and further we know that they have held this position for a very long period, since in the Book of Jesus ben Sirach, a Jewish writer who lived soon after 200 B.C., reference is made to the Book of Isaiah in terms which make it perfectly certain that it then included chs. xl. ff. The belief that these chapters are the composition of Isaiah, son of Amoz, has hardly been doubted, or indeed discussed, until recent times. But it is easy to see that in a case of this kind the traditional opinion, despite its great age, might be mistaken. The chapters themselves (unlike such passages as ch. vi. in the earlier part of the Book) contain *no* claim whatsoever to be the work of Isaiah, and the traditional ascription of them to him rests solely on the fact that they form part of a volume to which his name has been attached. That, however, is a circumstance which could arise in various ways. We know for certain that the prophetic books of the O.T. were not arranged in their present form by the prophets themselves but by later editors who collected all the remains of the prophetic literature which they were able to find and put them together in four great volumes— Isaiah, Jeremiah, Ezekiel, and the Minor Prophets (the last named being regarded by the later Jews as forming one book in the Hebrew O.T.). It might easily

happen that in this process the judgement of the
editors or compilers was sometimes at fault. If someone
found these twenty-seven chapters without any name
attached to them, various reasons might occur to him
inclining him to add them to the Isaiah collection—either
because he honestly but mistakenly believed them to be
Isaiah's, or (though this is a possibility we need not
seriously contemplate) because he wished to pass them
off as Isaiah's, knowing they were not his, or (and this is
the most probable reason) because their subject-matter
and style appeared to him such as to form a desirable
continuation to the group of prophecies containing Isaiah's
actual utterances.   Tradition, then, in this case is not
very strong to begin with, and of course it becomes no
stronger because it has been repeated from age to age.
It is not strong enough to give us an indisputable
assurance that here we are reading actual words of
Isaiah.   And since it is essential that we should en-
deavour to understand the situation in which the words
were written or spoken, it is a duty forced upon us to
investigate the tradition and see whether or not it puts us
at a point of view from which we can really enter into the
meaning of the prophecy.

But before proceeding to review this question, it is
right to refer to an argument which is sometimes used to
support this particular tradition and to rule out any attempt
to criticise its accuracy. It is pointed out that our Lord
and the N.T. writers generally shared the belief that
Isaiah wrote these chapters ; and from this the inference
is drawn that we must hold the same opinion on their
authority.   Our reply to this argument is that, whilst the
statement is correct, the conclusion is false. From such
passages as Matt. iii. 3, viii. 17, xii. 17, Luke iv. 17,
John i. 23, Acts viii. 28, Rom. x. 16, 20, it is clear that
in this question (as in other matters of secular knowledge)
our Lord and His disciples participated in the beliefs of

the period. But to assert in consequence that all such beliefs must be correct or else the religious value of the N.T. revelation would be impaired is a quite arbitrary assumption, which betrays a very serious misconception of the nature of our Lord's supreme authority. A glance at the passages cited above is sufficient to show that in no case does the truth which our Lord desired to enforce depend on whether the words quoted were uttered by Isaiah. Such questions as the one now before us cannot be determined except by a careful examination of all the facts.

II.

The Internal Evidence.

1. It is at once obvious that the prophecy is addressed to the people of Israel, but equally plain is the fact that a large number of Israelites are spoken of as living far from their native land of Palestine—most of them apparently in Babylonia, but others in various distant parts of the earth (see xliii. 6; xlv. 13; xlviii. 20; xlix. 5, 12, 21, 22; li. 11, 14; lii. 5; lvi. 8; lx. 4, 9; lxvi. 20). Moreover we find that these exiles, at any rate those in Babylonia, are there under compulsion from the rulers of the Babylonian Empire. They are involuntary exiles from their native land, subject to the tyranny of the race which has conquered them; and we may gather how hard their lot had been made from the wrathful terms in which the prophet refers to the proud and pitiless city of Babylon (ch. xlvii., esp. *v.* 6). There are also numerous indications of the fact that Jerusalem had suffered a disaster at some date now long past from which it had not yet recovered— the prophet speaks of it as a ruined city, 'desolate,' 'forgotten of Yahwe[1],' its Temple burnt with fire (e.g. xlix.

---

[1] This form of the Divine Name, now generally accepted as correct, will be used throughout the volume in place of the familiar rendering 'Jehovah,' which rests upon a mistaken transliteration of the Hebrew word.

14-21; li. 17-20; lii. 1, 2, 9; liv.). We know that this was not the case in the time of Isaiah. The exact date of his death has not been recorded. Tradition relates that he perished as a martyr in the reign of Manasseh, Hezekiah's unworthy successor. But in any case he can have known Judah only as an independent country, Jerusalem an unconquered city, and the Temple of Solomon an inviolate shrine. For the kingdom of Judah, although constantly menaced by the ambitions of the Northern Power, succeeded in maintaining itself as a separate state for more than a hundred years after the repulse of the Assyrian Sennacherib in 701 B.C., an event which was the climax of Isaiah's prophetical career.

Further we know exactly how and when just such a disaster overtook Jerusalem as is implied by the language of these chapters. In 607 B.C. the Assyrian Empire was conquered and its western territories acquired by the Babylonians. This change, however, in the controlling Power of the North only increased the peril of Judah, for the new Empire gave immediate proof of its strength by defeating in 605 B.C. a great Egyptian army, which had marched to Carchemish on the Euphrates. A few years later Judah began to be harassed by the Babylonian armies, and in 597 B.C. Nebuchadrezzar, the King of Babylon, with a great host advanced against Jerusalem, captured the city, and carried into captivity Jehoiachin, King of Judah, and the leading citizens. Finally in 587 B.C., in consequence of a foolish revolt in reliance on Egyptian help, Jerusalem was again attacked, taken, and sacked, its wall being destroyed and the famous Temple of Solomon burnt down. Most of the inhabitants were now deported to Babylonia, only the poorest being allowed to remain, and of these a large number shortly afterwards fled into Egypt. Here then we have that great national disaster, to which the author of Is. xl.-lxvi. looks back as an event of the past, at the same time declaring his prophetic conviction that the sad period of desolation and exile is on the point of ending. From this alone it is manifest that, whoever wrote this prophecy, it was not written regarding the men of Isaiah's time or addressed to their situation, but for a much later generation of Israelites, placed in such circumstances as would exist in the exilic period to which we have just referred.

2. We find in the next place that there are definite references in chs. xl. ff. to a great king and conqueror named Cyrus, who is declared by the prophet to be the destined agent of Yahwe in breaking the power of Babylon and setting the exiles free (see xliv. 28; xlv. 1–5; and cp. xli. 2, 3). Now in all history there is but one king named Cyrus, and fortunately we know a good deal about him although not all that we should like to know. The information we possess agrees perfectly with the allusions in the prophecy and helps us greatly to understand it. The name of Cyrus first appears on contemporary Babylonian inscriptions, where he is spoken of as King of Persia and Anzan, a state in Elam a country to the east of Babylon. In 549 B.C. he conquered Astyages, King of Media, becoming king of that country in his stead and thus founding the great power which was long known as the Medo-Persian Empire. The second stage in Cyrus' career was his defeat of Croesus, the King of Lydia, whose capital, Sardis, with its far-famed treasures fell into the conqueror's hands, 546 B.C. He next advanced against Babylon itself, which he entered in 538 B.C. after a short and almost bloodless campaign, for Nabonidus, the last of the Babylonian monarchs, had made himself extremely unpopular with his subjects and Cyrus was generally received as a liberator and benefactor. Such are the central and indisputable facts in a career which naturally startled the world by its unparalleled rapidity and success.

Beyond question, the features of chs. xl. ff. are in striking harmony with these events. Taken in conjunction with the circumstances set forth in paragraph 1, the two lines of evidence clearly indicate that the prophecy deals with the situation which existed in the exilic period of Jewish history shortly before 538 B.C.

3. But it may be urged that all this does not prove that these chapters were not written by Isaiah. Isaiah was a prophet, and might have foreseen the situation described and have written a book which would suit it when it came to pass. We do not deny that this is *possible*; but the task before us is not to decide what is possible, but first to weigh the evidence and form our opinion as to what actually happened. We shall then reply, that such a phenomenon would be absolutely without parallel in the records of prophecy. There are many cases, of course, in which a prophet makes a prediction or for a moment transports himself to some future time and speaks as if it were already present (e.g. Is. x. 28–32), but always with a view to instructing his contemporaries. Here, however,—on the supposition that Isaiah is the author,—his contemporaries are altogether ignored; he speaks not only *about* the future but *to* a far future generation and as if he were their contemporary.

Again the present case would in no way resemble the flashes of foresight or vivid imagination of the future found in other prophets. If Isaiah were the author we would here have an instance of a prophet not only transferring his whole consciousness to an imagined future (without a single lapse into his real present), but also from that standpoint forecasting a yet more distant future, supporting his arguments and rebukes by references to events in a past which was actually still future, and moving with perfect ease and naturalness in an imagined present, which confronts him with all the elements of a complex and quite definite historical situation. The astounding nature of this supposed *tour de force* is further heightened by the consideration that it is presented in a form quite

unlike that which we might have expected, were Isaiah
anticipating the future. Thus, for instance, we might
conceive him predicting—'Israel will be taken captive
and Jerusalem will become desolate, and after a certain
time a great conqueror [Cyrus] will arise and set Israel
free.' But here we are told 'Cyrus *has* arisen and is
shortly going to release Israel and at last Jerusalem
shall be rebuilt.' We must again remind the reader that
we are not discussing possibility but probability; and we
must insist that the supposed phenomenon is absolutely
improbable. We reject the theory that Isaiah in these
chapters is foreseeing the future not because it would be
marvellous, but because the theory does not really cover
the facts, and is totally opposed to the nature and inspiration of the prophetic writings.

4. The above considerations are sufficient by themselves to show that chs. xl. ff. were written by an unknown
prophet during the Babylonian captivity about 540 B.C.
But they are confirmed by others of a more intricate
nature which cannot be fully stated here. Each prophet
has an individuality of his own, which appears quite clearly
in the range of his ideas as well as in the style of his
writing and the vocabulary he employs. With regard to
range of ideas, we may notice that in Isaiah's acknowledged
prophecies the dominant note is warning, lest Israel should
incur the penalty of Yahwe's wrath, whereas in chs. xl. ff.
it is comfort, because the penalty has been borne and the
revelation of Yahwe's merciful pardon is now at hand.
Again, to Isaiah the righteousness of God signifies that
quality in the Divine Nature which will not tolerate injustice between man and man ; in this writer it denotes in
the first place Yahwe's faithfulness in His purpose of
redemption, and then it passes into the concrete meaning of the status of salvation, and so salvation itself.
There is agreement that Yahwe is supreme, but whilst
Isaiah does not dwell on the might of Yahwe as Creator

of Nature and of Man, the author of chs. xl. ff. makes that doctrine a fundamental factor in his argument. The conceptions of the Remnant and of the Messiah, prominent in chs. i.–xxxix., vanish in chs. xl. ff., and the destiny of Israel is set forth under the figure of the Servant of Yahwe and in a way that implies a quite different expectation concerning the ideal age which is to come. Moreover, the relation of Israel to the Gentiles in chs. xl. ff. expresses a note of universalist sympathy, which transcends the point of view reached by Isaiah. Thus, in chs. xl. ff. the ancient belief (shared by Isaiah) that Israel is the chosen people of God is maintained in strong, perhaps hyperbolical, terms (xliii. 3). But this prophet, with wonderful religious insight, further perceives that the privilege of Israel is but the measure of her responsibility. Not that He may pamper Zion has Yahwe chosen her, but in order that in her history, that is in His dealings with her, the character of the true God may be convincingly displayed.

Turning to the question of literary style we find a no less significant distinction. The utterances of Isaiah have the tone of public pronouncements, are couched in forcible and concise style, and deal with ever-varying themes, whereas the prophecy of chs. xl. ff. is remarkable for the impassioned reiteration of a few favourite thoughts, which are expanded in stately, imaginative language. The one prophet is a commanding orator, the other a persuasive poet. Various minor characteristics may be mentioned as typical of the style of chs. xl. ff. :—duplication of words or phrases (xl. 1 ; xliii. 11, 25; li. 9, 12, 17); descriptive clauses added to the Name of God or of Israel (xl. 28 f.; xli. 8; xliv. 24–28); frequent use of rhetorical questions (xl. *passim* ; xliv. 7, 8, 10); and peculiarly vivid personification (see esp. lii. 13–liii. 12). This general impression as to the style is overwhelmingly supported by a minute examination of the vocabulary employed. It must here suffice to say that chs. xl. ff. both lack the characteristic expressions found in Isaiah and are themselves characterised by a different set of words and phrases (esp. particles). So great is the contrast in this respect that a change of author is clearly implied.

5. Having thus determined the age of the prophecy and its author (whom for convenience we may term II Isaiah), we may go on to inquire into a less important point, viz. the *place* where he lived and wrote. Here we shall find ourselves unable to reach so positive a conclusion. Both Egypt and Phoenicia have been suggested as the place of composition; but the evidence is very slender, and both these localities may be ruled out. There is strong evidence in favour of Babylonia as the place of origin, especially as regards chs. xl.–xlviii. Thus, besides the references to Babylon and its interests, it may be argued that the stress laid on idols and image-making, sorcery, and astrology, as well as the keen interest shown in the progress of Cyrus, favour Babylonian surroundings. Important also is the close resemblance between Is. xliv. 27–xlv. 3 and the official Babylonian style, as exemplified in the inscriptions of Cyrus.

But to all these points an answer can be given, and a strong case made out for Palestinian origin. Granting that the prophet (II Isaiah) does appeal to the exiles in Babylon, it does not follow that he is resident among them. His plea may be uttered from Jerusalem, and indeed such passages as xli. 9, xliii. 6, lii. 7, 11, seem to imply this, although it is of course open to those who maintain the Babylonian origin to reply that the prophet in those verses is but imagining himself to be in Palestine. Moreover it is undeniable that his exhortations and encouragements are often addressed directly to Jerusalem and that they are eminently suitable to the situation of its despairing population, sighing for the return of the

Israelites exiled and scattered throughout many lands though chiefly in the territories of the Babylonian tyrant.

Again it may be urged that the strong Babylonian colouring, with which the Book of Ezekiel (certainly composed in Babylon) is impregnated, is reduced in chs. xl. ff. to just such general references and feelings as would naturally result from the Babylonian domination of Palestine. The strongest argument, however, for the Palestinian origin of these chapters is that the illustrations and phraseology, esp. in chs. xlix. ff. but *also* in xl.–xlviii., reflect in the most natural fashion the agricultural conditions of Palestine. We must not pursue the subject further, although a great deal more may be said on both sides. For the time being, the matter must be considered an open question. Not a few commentators hold that chs. xlix.–lxvi. are Palestinian, whilst xl.–xlviii. are Babylonian. The present writer inclines to the belief that undue weight has been given to the supposed indications of Babylonian origin, and that even chs. xl.–xlviii. may be the work of a prophet resident in Jerusalem.

There is general agreement that chs. lvi.–lxvi. were composed in Palestine (see § 6 *c*, below).

6. One other question of this kind demands consideration. Is the prophecy a unity ? Was it all written by one man and at one time, or was its composition spread over many years and does it perhaps combine writings of several prophets? At the end of ch. xlviii. and of ch. lvii. there occur the words 'There is no peace, saith the Lord, to the wicked,' and the same sentiment is expressed by the last verse of ch. lxvi., a fact which naturally gave rise to the supposition that the author intended the prophecy to fall into three parts of nine chapters each. But the theory fails to stand the test of careful consideration, which reveals that there is no real break between chs. lvi. and lvii., and that the real division is rather chs. xl.–xlviii., xlix.–lv., and lvi.–lxvi. (see §§ *b*, *c*, below).

Apart from the fact that occasional glosses have been added by later editors and copyists, the unity of chs. xl.–lxvi. may be questioned in respect of the following portions.

(*a*) Four wonderful passages, known as the Servant-songs (xlii. 1–4; xlix. 1–6; l. 4–9; lii. 13–liii. 12), present a deeper conception of the Servant of Yahwe than is found in the other passages where the title is used. Whether the difference is due to a change of author depends largely on the view taken as to the personality of the Servant in the four Servant-songs (see pp. xxvii ff.), and is indeed a question so intricate that it cannot adequately be discussed here. It is certain that in all other passages except these four the Servant is a title denoting the nation of Israel. If therefore the opinion that in the Servant-songs the Servant denotes an individual be correct, a difference of authorship would seem highly probable, since the same writer would surely not use the same title in different senses without any indication of the change. If on the other hand the Servant personifies the nation of Israel in some sense in these four Songs just as elsewhere in the prophecy, the problem is more difficult. Against the view that the Songs have been inserted by a later author is the difficulty of seeing any reason why they have been separated one from another and assigned to the particular positions in which they now stand. Moreover we should expect, if the Songs were interpolations, to be able to detect in the context the 'hand' of the editor who inserted them. Now, when the verses which immediately follow the Songs, and are supposed to be linking verses inserted by the editor, are closely scrutinised, they are seen to have the precise form and style of II Isaiah's acknowledged writings and to disclose such subtle points of connection with his thought that altogether they cannot plausibly be regarded as the work of an editor. It is therefore probable that the Songs were written by II Isaiah himself, or possibly by an earlier prophet, whose work II Isaiah has adapted and incorporated with his own utterances. The former view is preferable, and, even if the latter were true, it is clear that the passages now form part of II Isaiah's teaching and 'for all practical purposes may be treated as if they were his own work.'

(*b*) There is a distinct alteration of theme and of outlook between chs. xl.–xlviii. and xlix.–lv., for with ch. xlix. the denunciations of Babylon and its idols and the references to Cyrus cease, whilst the central idea changes from the comforting of Israel, the nation, to the comforting of Jerusalem, Israel's city (see further the head-note to ch. xlix.). There is, however, hardly any perceptible change of style or vocabulary, and the two sections are significantly united by the 'golden thread' of the Servant-songs, three of which occur in chs. xlix.–lv. The difference in the subject-matter may therefore be regarded as sufficiently accounted for by the supposition that chs. xlix.–lv. were composed by II Isaiah somewhat later than chs. xl.–xlviii. (If chs. xl.–xlviii. were composed in Babylon, and xlix.–lv. in Palestine [see p. xviii f.], we must suppose that II Isaiah returned to Palestine with the first band of released exiles, about 537 B.C., shortly after the accession of Cyrus.)

(*c*) Much more important are the features which distinguish chs. lvi.–lxvi. from xl.–lv. An analysis of these last eleven chapters of the Book shows that they consist of a number of separate or very loosely connected utterances, having for the most part some general resemblance to one another, but differing from chs. xl.–lv. in style, ideas, and historical outlook. For details the reader is referred to the notes on these chapters, pp. 83 ff. Many features combine to establish a very strong probability that the author (or authors) of these passages confronts the problems and needs of the post-exilic community in Jerusalem about 460–450 B.C., nearly a hundred years after the period to which we assign the writings of II Isaiah, and shortly before the advent of Nehemiah and Ezra. The standpoint of the prophet is certainly Jerusalem, but a Jerusalem in which the Temple has been restored (an event which we know definitely was brought about in the years 518–516 B.C.), although the walls of the city still remain unbuilt. It is true that the style and thought of one section (viz. chs. lx.–lxii.) bear the closest resemblance to the writing of II Isaiah, esp. in ch. liv. ; but there are certain points of detail which seem to imply that even this passage belongs to the later date. The other sections of lvi.–lxvi. are differentiated from the work of II Isaiah by profound divergences of style, ideas, and feeling, whilst the resemblances or reminiscences which can be traced are only such as would be accounted for by supposing that the author of these sections had known and admired the utterances of his great predecessor.

III.

THE TEACHING OF THE BOOK.

Having thus reached the conclusion that Is. xl.–lxvi. is the work of a prophet (or prophets) of whose career we know only that he (or they) wrote these chapters at a certain period of history and to people in clearly defined circumstances, we have next to inquire into the purpose and leading ideas of the prophecy. What does the writer (we shall use the singular) chiefly wish to impress on his audience, or to teach them, or call on them to do ? In a word, what is the message of the book?

1. The first thing that strikes us is that the prophet is eager to impress on his countrymen a due sense of the majesty, the power, the incomparableness of Yahwe, the God of Israel, who is the only true and living God. This prophet is perhaps the greatest monotheist of the O.T. At least it is he who has most adequately brought out and

most eloquently expatiated upon, the doctrine of the unity and omnipotence of God. The idea of Yahwe as the Creator and Ruler of the Universe is set forth in splendid language. By His unaided wisdom and power (see esp. xl. 12–26) He created and controls the stars in the heavens (xl. 26; xlv. 12,18), the earth with its mountains and seas (xl. 12 ; li. 10), and all living creatures, both man and beast (xlii. 5). By His will the face of Nature may be transformed in the most wonderful fashion (xli. 18, 19 ; l. 2, 3). Existent from eternity (xl. 28; xliv. 6), supreme in knowledge and power, He can foresee and direct the development of human history. Providence is but the unfolding of His will. No combination of men and nations, no matter how powerful they may seem, will be able to prevent the realisation of His purposes (xl. 23, 24). But, if the opposition of human enemies is vain, what of the gods whom the heathen nations worship? No help, the prophet declares, can be found in these so-called deities and their images. Upon the folly of worshipping idols, the work of men's hands, mere pieces of wood and stone, the prophet pours ironical scorn (xl. 19, 20 ; xli. 7 ; xliv. 9–20 ; xlvi. 6, 7). As for the beings whom these images are supposed to represent, they are nonentities, creations of the human imagination, powerless to work good or evil. The question is brought to a dramatic issue, the test chosen being the capacity for making successful prediction. In answer to the challenge of Yahwe it appears that the idols and their worshippers can cite no instance of verified prediction and are unable to foretell the events now about to happen (xli. 21–24 ; xliii. 9), whereas Yahwe, with Israel as His witness, can triumphantly point to former prophecies fulfilled (xliv. 8 ; xlviii. 6, 7) as a guarantee that the promises now uttered will also be proved true.

When the impotence of the false gods is thus set in contrast with the omnipotence and omniscience of

Yahwe, it is no wonder that the prophet loves to enforce the thought of His uniqueness: He is Yahwe, the incomparable (xl. 25 ; xlv. 18, 21 ; xlvi. 5), the ' Holy One ' (as alone possessing the attributes of true divinity), the ' First and the Last, beside whom there is no God ' (xli. 4 ; xliv. 6 ; xlviii. 12).

2. Another element of fundamental importance in the teaching of the prophet is his view of the character of God. For if the Almighty has at His disposal infinite resources of wisdom and power, it is of the essence of any truly religious message that it should contain a clear declaration of the purpose to which these resources will be applied ; and that must depend on the character of the Being who controls them. The prophet declares that the omnipotent Yahwe is a Being of morally perfect character. This conviction he expresses for the most part by dwelling upon the righteousness of Yahwe. The term is used with a depth or a width of meaning which cannot be fully stated here. As regards Yahwe it denotes fundamentally the quality of trustworthiness, reliability, faithfulness to a purpose, self-consistency in word and deed. His righteousness therefore is displayed in every act which conduces to the execution of His object. And since His object is the deliverance of Israel and, ultimately, the salvation of all mankind, the idea of Yahwe's righteousness comes into vital relationship with the thought of His redemptive power. Yahwe is 'a just and saving God' (xlv. 21), the only 'Saviour' (xliii. 11). In fact so inevitably is 'redemption,' 'salvation,' the result of Yahwe's righteousness, that in certain passages (e.g. xlvi. 13 ; li. 6, 8) 'righteousness' denotes not the attribute but its actual outcome, i.e. 'victory,' 'success.'

The prophet also emphasises another aspect of Yahwe's moral perfection—namely, His wonderful tenderness. His care for Israel exceeds that of a mother for her infant child (xlix. 14, 15 ; cp. lxvi. 13); like a shepherd He will

lead home His people with the most compassionate
regard even for the weakest of the flock (xl. 11) ; and,
above all, His wrath will be seen to have lasted but 'for
a moment' when compared with the everlasting mercy
which is now to be revealed (liv. 8).

3. The central message of the prophet is that this
Almighty, faithful, and merciful God is about to sum up
human history in a final manifestation of His glory, by a
series of stupendous physical and political convulsions
which will result in the triumphant restoration of the
exiled people of Israel to their own land, and, eventually,
in the joyful acceptance of the true religion by all nations
of the earth.   Repeatedly it is predicted that the desert
lands are about to experience a transformation into
fertility and beauty as a preparation for the march of the
exiled Israelites, whom Yahwe Himself will lead back to
their ancient home (xl. 3, 4 ; xli. 17-19 ; xlii. 14-16 ;
xliii. 19, 20 ; xlix. 9-12). The political 'sign of the times'
is to be found in the career of Cyrus, who is declared
to be unconsciously the agent of Yahwe's purpose—raised
up and sustained by His resistless will (xli. 2, 3 ; xlv. 1-6),
and destined shortly to conquer Babylon itself (cp. xlvii. ;
xliii. 14 ; xlvi. 1, 2), to set free the captive Israelites, and to
command the restoration of Jerusalem (xliv. 28).   At
Yahwe's bidding the peoples of north and south and east
and west will give up the exiled Israelites (xliii. 5, 6 ;
xlix. 12, 22), who will return through the transformed
deserts to the joys of a restored and glorified Jerusalem
(li. 3 ; lii.-lv. *passim* ; cp. lx., lxii.). Finally, the nations,
overcome by this amazing spectacle, will be convinced of
the folly of their idolatrous worship, and will eagerly
come, in humility and penitence, to be taught by Israel
the knowledge of the one true God (xlv. 14, 22-24).

4. But the prophet's inspiration reaches a yet higher level
in his conception of the religious mission of the people of
Israel.   Not only is Israel's restoration and exaltation to

be to all the world a proof of the glory of Yahwe, the God
of Israel, and of His universal supremacy, but Israel itself
is to be the means of converting the world and instructing
it in the true knowledge of God.   This idea is developed
by the prophet through the lofty conception of the *Servant
of Yahwe*.   It is quite impossible in this place to discuss
fully the problems which arise in connection with this
title, as even to summarise the present trend and balance
of opinion.   All that can be done is to indicate in a few
words the main facts regarding the phrase and its
religious significance in II Isaiah.

(*a*) *The Servant of Yahwe.* On the one hand there are
a number of passages (e.g. xli. 8; xlii. 19, 20 ; xliv. 1 f. ;
xlv. 4) in which there can be no question that the title
'Servant of Yahwe' denotes the historic nation of
Israel. Even we are accustomed, in such a phrase as
'England expects every man to do his duty,' to personify
the nation, and speak of it as an individual.   But the
orientals, and especially the Hebrews, carried this ten-
dency much further than is natural for us, and could
freely speak of a nation as born, acting in a personal
manner, dying, rising from the dead, and so forth.   So
far there arises no difficulty, the only question being *in
what sense* is the historic people of Israel termed the
Lord's Servant.   Doubtless Israel might be called Yahwe's
Servant simply because it acknowledged Him as its God.
But an examination of the passages where the title is
used shows that the prophet has a deeper meaning in
mind. He lays stress upon the peculiar privilege of Israel
in having been specially 'called,' 'chosen,' 'created' by
Yahwe, as though implying that Israel has some signal
mission to fulfil for its God.   In xlii. 19, it is acknowledged
that Israel has been blind and deaf in the execution of this
mission.   Nevertheless, though it has remained passive
and unconscious of its duty, Yahwe has caused it to be
instrumental in achieving His purpose ; for He has made

its history a revelation of His character. Thus its misfortunes and sufferings reveal the consequences of sinning against the moral law and thereby display Yahwe's perfect ethical holiness, whilst the coming prosperity of Israel will manifest in equally signal fashion His faithfulness and His mercy. From this point of view, then, it may truly be said that Israel is His *witness* unto the peoples of the earth. In all this, however, it is obvious that the Servant is conceived as serving Yahwe, not so much actively as passively ; he has been, as it were, a mirror in which the attitude of God to man is clearly but mechanically reflected. There is, at any rate, no suggestion that the Servant has a mission towards the world which must be accomplished by positive, purposeful action.

(*b*) *The Suffering Servant.* On the other hand there are some passages—four in particular—which have long been singled out by scholars and, for convenience, entitled the 'Servant-songs' or 'Servant-passages' (viz. xlii. 1–4 ; xlix. 1–6 ; l. 4–9 ; lii. 13–liii. 12), in which a healing and enlightening mission to the whole world is clearly assigned to the Servant ; and in these the Servant is portrayed, not as 'blind and deaf' to his duty (cp. above), but as willing, active, blameless, and indefatigable in faithful pursuance of his high calling, which has brought upon him scorn, suffering, and even death itself. From this last of evils, however, Yahwe will presently deliver him by restoring his life, and, in reward for his integrity, will grant him to see the success of his work. It is evident that the ideal of the Servant in these four passages is profoundly different from that presented elsewhere. Whether the distinction is due to a difference of authorship has already been discussed (see p. xx f.). There is room for very great diversity of opinion on the questions here involved. The whole subject is immensely complicated by the fact that many readers feel these four passages to be so highly individual in their colouring that they

cannot believe the 'Suffering Servant' is a mere personification of the nation ; they hold that he is a real person,
and not Israel at all.

How to decide between these conflicting impressions is
the much-discussed problem of the Servant of the Lord in
II Isaiah. So baffling and intricate is the evidence both
for and against the various solutions which have been
proposed, that we cannot do more than indicate the main
lines of thought.

i. We may start from the impression that in these four
passages the Servant is an individual, and maintain either
that the prophet, who elsewhere uses the title as the
equivalent of Israel, on these four occasions has deliberately
employed it with a different significance, or else that the
change of meaning is to be explained by a change of
author. Both these explanations are open to serious
criticism, and further the 'individual' theory of the
Servant is exposed to the following objections. (*a*) In
xlix. 3, the Servant is expressly called 'Israel,' and no
convincing reason has been given to show that the
word is not part of the original text. (*b*) The idea of
a personal resurrection, such as is predicted for the
Servant in liii. 10-13, is improbable in the light of what
we know of the growth in the O.T. of belief in individual
immortality. (*c*) The *rôle* of the Servant, his world-wide
mission, and his unique relation to Yahwe, are of a quite
different order to the expectations which the prophets
entertained of any, even the greatest, individual men.
(*d*) The difficulty of identifying the Servant with
any known person has hitherto proved insuperable.
Neither Jeremiah, nor Zerubbabel or Jehoiachin (as
Davidic King), nor an unknown teacher of the Law in the
time of Nehemiah, nor yet Eleazar, a martyr in the
persecutions of Antiochus Epiphanes—fits all the requirements of the part. The one interpretation of this class
which must always be treated with respect is that the

Servant represents an ideal individual who shall appear in the future, the Messiah presented in a new and profoundly impressive aspect. It is, of course, true that, from the Christian standpoint, the ideal figure of the Servant did find full and final realisation in the person of Jesus Christ ; and we may legitimately measure the height of the prophet's spiritual nature by 'the marvellous degree in which he has been enabled to foreshadow the essential truths concerning the life and mission of the Redeemer'; but this fact does not give us the right to conclude that the person of Jesus Christ or any Messianic figure was the idea present in the mind of the prophet in delineating the character and work of the ideal Servant. However attractive that view may appear, it meets with a great and seemingly fatal objection in the numerous direct statements according to which it is evident that much of the Servant's career—his humiliation, suffering, and death—is regarded by the prophet as *already* past : only his resurrection and triumph belong to the future.

ii. Or we may start from what is quite certain—namely that the title does *sometimes* in chs. xl. ff. denote Israel, and say that it must bear the same meaning throughout : that the ideal Servant of the four Servant-songs still represents the *nation of Israel*, although the personification is carried much further than in the other passages where the title is employed. This theory is supported by many considerations, amongst which we may single out the fact that in xlix. 3 and xlii. 1 (Septuagint[1]) the Servant is definitely named 'Israel' (see the note to xlix. 3). On the other hand it is opposed by these two difficulties, first, that the ideal elements of the Suffering Servant's character, his patience, humility, innocence, and faithfulness, appear too sublime to be applicable to the disappointing career of historical Israel ; and, second, that in three verses (xlix. 5, 6 ; liii. 8) a distinction seems to be made between the

[1] Hereafter referred to by the abbreviation, LXX.

Servant and Israel as a whole. (It should, however, be noted that the evidence, on which this second objection is based, is by no means certain. Several scholars believe that the words in question are capable of a different meaning, and that the apparent distinction disappears as a mere misinterpretation of the Hebrew : see the notes on liii. 1–10, esp. *v.* 8 ; and xlix. 5, 6.)

Accordingly various modifications of the theory have been proposed. Thus it is suggested that the Suffering Servant typifies an *Ideal Israel* ; but if by this phrase is meant an abstract idea existent only in the hopes of the prophet, the solution is open to the fatal objection that it does not leave room for the statements that the Servant has undergone historical experiences : e.g. his past sufferings and death. Strong though the element of idealisation is, the picture does not seem to be entirely sundered from concrete reality.

Nor is it quite convincing to hold that the Servant personifies the *righteous section* of the nation. This view is attractive because, as is natural, many features of the Servant's character and career correspond with the experiences of the prophets and saints within Israel. But the unambiguous assertion of the Servant's death (liii. 8), which according to Hebrew thought is a quite natural metaphor to denote the loss of national independence at the time of the Exile, becomes hard to understand if applied merely to the righteous persons in Israel, for they did not actually die out at the Exile or any other period. Equally great, in the opinion of many scholars, is the difficulty of supposing that the righteous in Israel were singled out for such scorn and persecution as could account for the language of ch. liii., at least at any period early enough to be suitable. The terrible sufferings of certain faithful Jews in the Maccabean period might conceivably have called forth such senti- ments as are found in ch. liii. ; but, whether this opinion be justified or not, the date (*circa* 170–165 B.C.) is too late to make an identification of the Servant with those martyrs at all probable. And, in general, the notion that the Servant is only the spiritual kernel of the nation, imposes an undesirable limitation upon the idealism of the writer. ' Like all prophets of the O.T. he operates with nations and peoples. And if the nations are to receive "light" through Israel, it will be through Israel, again an imposing people before the world's eyes.'

iii. Each of these aspects, taken separately, is open to objections more or less serious, yet all reflect features present in the wonderful picture of the Servant of the Lord. It remains to consider whether they ought not somehow to be combined. May it not be that the Servant represents Israel, not in some sense, but in many senses ; that the Servant is always ' Israel,' and that the complex features in his personality may be accounted for by fluctuations in the aspect under which the prophet happens to be thinking of his people? In the present writer's opinion this is on the whole the best interpretation to put on the apparent contradictions of the existing text. We could then maintain that, in passages other than the four Servant-songs, the prophet has in mind the character and career of the whole nation as it had actually existed in history. If so, then it is natural that the Servant should there be represented as deaf and disobedient, yet not wholly cast off and not wholly useless. On the other hand, in the Servant-songs he is thinking of Israel as it should be, a perfect Israel, the nation as it is in the mind and purpose of God. Not that the prophet regards this conception of Israel as an abstract ideal, quite unrealised in actual life. He means by it real, historical Israel—but Israel seen in the light of his inspired optimism. Just as a Christian to-day might think or write of the ideal Church of Christ as really existent in the actual historical churches despite their imperfections now and in the past, so there was a way of looking at the actual people of Israel which enabled the prophet to feel that the perfect Israel was more than an unrealised dream. It had had some historical embodiment in the faithful members of the nation, who, though numerically a part, might be thought of as ideally the whole nation, the true Israel, the faithful Servant. This would leave room for the inclusion of historical experiences in the Servant's past career; whilst we could also maintain that the Servant does not typify a pious minority in the nation, but is indeed the whole people, ideally considered. Finally, if the three verses, liii. 8, xlix. 5, 6, do really imply a distinction between Israel and the Servant, we might answer this objection by insisting on the fact that in such a conception of the Servant as has just been indicated an element of paradox was natural and only to be expected : looking forward to the Servant's universal mission the prophet would see an Israel perfect in all its members, looking back upon the actual chequered past he would see not merely the rebellious sin-stained people, a very imperfect Servant, but also—such is the triumph of his faith—the presence of the Ideal Israel, personified at least in the persons of those who, in the face of all opposition, patiently and heroically, had maintained amongst their brethren the knowledge and worship of the one true God.

IV.

THE RELIGIOUS VALUE.

Whatever be the opinion we may prefer to hold upon these difficult literary and historical questions, it is right that in conclusion we should emphasise the value of the ideal portrayed in the figure of the Suffering Servant. How can such a life and death as his be reconciled with the belief that the world is controlled by a gracious and all powerful God ? The prophet faces this mystery as it appeared in the sufferings of his nation at the hands of its ruthless and idolatrous oppressors. He finds an answer in the thought that, in the purpose of God, Israel is called to be—the Prophet of the Gentiles. As such, her tribulations seemed but the counterpart of the persecution endured by the prophets *within* Israel; and the life of such a man as Jeremiah was sufficient proof that ignominy and suffering might be willingly accepted in the task of leading Israel to know and serve its God. Moreover the *redemptive* power of such a life was manifest beyond dispute: the blood of the prophets had been the life of their people. And this fact was enough to sustain the prophet's faith in God, and to lead him on to the conviction that ultimately—though the fashion of it transcends our human imagination—God would not fail to vindicate His Servant. Now the origin of new religious truth is in personal experience, and we may be sure that the writer shared in the heroic spirit of the prophets, and knew something of their pain. Hence, although we see that the teaching of these chapters was uttered primarily in regard to the life of the nation, it may with justice be applied to the experiences of the individual. The picture of the Suffering Servant is more than an intellectual feat; it is a victory of faith achieved in the stress of life.

Taking chs. xl.–lxvi. as a whole, we may say that the faith which pervades them is based on the conviction that God has a kingdom of righteousness and love to establish, first in Israel but finally among all nations; that He seeks the cooperation of men as His servants; and that in the end His purpose shall be accomplished, for His power is measureless and His mercy everlasting.

CHRONOLOGICAL TABLE

B.C.

597. Capture of Jerusalem by Nebuchadrezzar.

587. Fall of Jerusalem, and deportation of Jews to Babylon.

(Prophecies of Jeremiah: in Jerusalem 625–587 B.C., and afterwards in Egypt.)

(Prophecies of Ezekiel: in Babylon 593–570 B.C.

549. Cyrus becomes King of Media.

546. Cyrus conquers Croesus, and captures Sardis.

538. Cyrus enters Babylon, and establishes the Persian Empire.

537. Decree of Cyrus, permitting the exiles to return to Jerusalem.

529. Cambyses, King of the Persian Empire.

521. Darius I (Hystaspis).

(Prophecies of Haggai and Zechariah, 520–518 B.C.)

520–516. Building of the second Temple.

458–432. Reforms of Ezra and Nehemiah at Jerusalem.

331. Destruction of the Persian Empire by Alexander the Great.

323. Partition of Alexander's Empire among his generals; Ptolemy obtaining Egypt, and Seleucus Syria.

323–303. Palestine under Egyptian rule.

203–166. Jerusalem under Syrian rule.

168. Desecration of the Temple by Antiochus Epiphanes, King of Syria.

166–165. Revolt of the Jews, and victories of Judas Maccabaeus: the Temple reconsecrated.

ISAIAH

xl.–lv. A Gospel of Restoration: The Comforting of Israel.

xl.–lv. These chapters are a message of comfort and en couragement for Israel. They may be described as a Gospel, for they declare the good news that God has forgiven His people and will grant the blessings of salvation to Israel first, and then, through Israel, to all nations.

The principal topics are the omnipotence of Yahwe, the one real God, contrasted with the impotence of the false gods ; the election of Israel to be His servant, and its approaching deliverance through the victories of Cyrus, His chosen agent ; the triumphant return of Israel to Jerusalem under the guidance of its God ; the renewed glory of Zion-Jerusalem; and an explanation of the nation's past sufferings in the light of its destiny to win for Yahwe the adoration of all mankind. These subjects are not arranged in one progressive logical sequence. On the contrary one of the outstanding features of the prophecy is the constant repetition of the favourite themes with little variation of vocabulary or treatment. The writer is an anonymous prophet, generally called Second- or Deutero-Isaiah (II Isaiah) ; ahd the date of composition falls probably between 546 and 538 B.C. See the Introduction.

xl. 1–11. *The Prelude.* In these opening verses the dominant note of the prophecy is heard. Israel is forgiven and its restoration is at hand (*vv.* 1, 2). Long years of weakness and degradation have reduced it to despair, and there are many who declare that Yahwe has utterly abandoned His people (see *v.* 27). But the prophet, whose heart is attuned to hear the despair of Israel, is also in sympathy with the mind of God. For him the Divine silence is at last broken, and he hears the sound of heavenly voices proclaiming the mercy and the blessings which Yahwe will now bestow on His people. A first voice heralds Yahwe's advent, and commands that preparations be made by certain heavenly Beings for His royal progress through the deserts to Jerusalem (*vv.* 3–5). A second voice bids the prophet proclaim the transience of man and the eternal majesty of Israel's God (*vv.* 6–8). Thirdly, a command is given that messengers shall announce to Zion the approach of Yahwe, the omnipotent protector and the tender shepherd of His people (*vv.* 9–11).

xl. 1–11. The restoration proclaimed to Israel.

40   Comfort ye, comfort ye my people, saith your God.

2 Speak ye comfortably to Jerusalem, and cry unto her,
that her warfare is accomplished, that her iniquity is
pardoned; that she hath received of the LORD'S hand
double for all her sins.

3   The voice of one that crieth, Prepare ye in the wilderness the way of the LORD, make straight in the desert

---

1.   Comfort ye, comfort ye: note the repetition, a feature
characteristic of the prophet's style. The command is addressed
to all who love Jerusalem and can hear the heavenly voice.

2.   comfortably to: lit. 'to the heart of,' i.e. tenderly, kindly:
cp. Ruth ii. 13; Jud. xix. 3; Gen. l. 21.

Jerusalem: although the best part of the nation was dispersed
among the Gentiles in Babylon and Egypt, yet the hope of Israel
still centred in the ancient capital. Its name, Jerusalem or Zion,
became the symbol of racial and religious unity.   Here it is
used as the equivalent of 'my people' (*v.* 1).   If Jerusalem
remained unblessed, Israel could not be comforted.

warfare: marg. 'time of service.'   Originally a military
expression, the word acquired a wider significance, denoting
any period of severe, painful, toil (cp. Job vii. 1).   In the
present instance, the reference is to the sufferings of Jerusalem
during the exilic period.

iniquity: or 'penalty.'   The word denotes not merely guilt
but also its consequence, punishment.

is pardoned: rather 'her penalty is discharged' (worked off).
Israel's sufferings have at last paid off the debt incurred by its
past sinfulness.   Its punishment is accounted adequate by the
mercy which seasons the Divine justice.

double: an emphatic way of saying that the penalty has
been sufficient.   There can be no intention of suggesting that
God has been unjustly severe.

3.   The voice…crieth: 'Hark! one crying.'   From the
pronoun 'our' at the end of the verse, it is clear that the
speaker is not God Himself, whilst the superhuman nature
of the task enjoined implies that the voice is not that of a man.
We must infer that it is an angelic Being who commands his
fellows to prepare the miraculous path in the deserts.

in the wilderness: the A.V. (following the LXX and quotations
in the N.T.) punctuates wrongly '…crieth in the wilderness,
Prepare ye….'   The R.V. is correct.

make straight: rather, as marg., 'level.'

a high way for our God. Every valley shall be exalted, 4
and every mountain and hill shall be made low: and
the crooked shall be made straight, and the rough
places plain: and the glory of the LORD shall be re- 5
vealed, and all flesh shall see it together: for the mouth
of the LORD hath spoken it. The voice of one saying, 6
Cry. And one said, What shall I cry? All flesh is
grass, and all the goodliness thereof is as the flower
of the field: the grass withereth, the flower fadeth; 7
because the breath of the LORD bloweth upon it: surely
the people is grass. The grass withereth, the flower 8
fadeth: but the word of our God shall stand for ever.

O thou that tellest good tidings to Zion, get thee up into 9

---

4. and the crooked...plain: better 'the rugged land shall
become a plain, and the mountain-passes a valley.' The
language is not wholly metaphorical. Whatever would obstruct
the path of the returning exiles, natural as well as political
hindrances, will be smoothed away by the power of God.

5. This verse is the climax of the proclamation uttered by
the first voice. It may be noted that the phrase 'for the mouth
of the Lord hath spoken it' is not used elsewhere by II Isaiah;
but cp. Is. lviii. 14, also Is. i. 20, and Mic. iv. 4.

6. The voice...saying: 'Hark! one saying.' A second
angelic voice, addressing the prophet, now commands him to
proclaim the transience of man and the eternity of God.

And one said: better, as marg., 'And I said.'

7. the breath...Lord: the prophet may have in mind the
scorching winds, which, 'laden with a mist of fine sand,'
blow over Palestine from the deserts and often ruin the spring
vegetation.

surely...grass: 'the people' is normally used by this writer
to mean Israel; but in this context it must denote 'humanity,'
and, in particular, Israel's oppressors whom God will destroy
like grass. Since the phrase disturbs the metre and is a prosaic
explanation of 'all flesh is grass,' it is probably a gloss.

8. the word of our God: the glory of human plans and achieve-
ments vanishes. Nothing abides except that which is effected
by the Word of God, i.e. by the expression of His immutable
will. The good news of *vv.* 1, 2, is therefore certain of
fulfilment.

9. O thou...Zion: lit. 'Herald of good news to Zion,' but
the word 'herald' is collective, 'a band of messengers,'

the high mountain; O thou that tellest good tidings to Jerusalem, lift up thy voice with strength; lift it up, be not afraid; say unto the cities of Judah, Behold, your 10 God! Behold, the Lord GOD will come as a mighty one, and his arm shall rule for him: behold, his reward is with 11 him, and his recompence before him. He shall feed his flock like a shepherd, he shall gather the lambs in his arm, and carry them in his bosom, *and* shall gently lead those that give suck.

12-31. *The incomparable might of Yahwe.*
12-17. *His rule over Nature.*

12 Who hath measured the waters in the hollow of his hand, and meted out heaven with the span, and com-

---

doubtless those who carry out the command of *vv.* 1, 2. Another rendering (LXX and A.V.) is ' Zion, herald of good news,' as if Jerusalem is to proclaim the tidings to the surrounding territory. Both translations are sound grammatically, but only the first is probable, being supported by xli. 27, lii. 7.

be not afraid: lest events should play their hopes false.

10. Probably the prophet is now the speaker, not the angel messengers.

will come...one: or perhaps ' cometh in might.'

his arm: the symbol of His controlling power, cp. xlviii. 14; li. 9; lii. 10.

his reward: (1) the blessings God will bestow on His restored people, or possibly (2) the exiles themselves, regarded as spoil captured from the Gentile nations.

11. A verse of wonderful beauty, cp. Jer. xxxi. 10; Ezek. xxxiv. 11-16. To His enemies Yahwe is omnipotence, to His own He reveals Himself as a God of infinite tenderness.

12-31. Faith is not easily renewed. Despite the closing assurance of the prologue that God's grace extends even to the weak and helpless, many in Israel are overawed by the apparent power of the gods of the heathen empires. Is Yahwe really their superior or even their equal? Let the prophet give a reason for the faith that is in him. In reply he contrasts the dominion of the true God over Nature (*vv.* 12-17) with the futility of the idols (*vv.* 18-20), and then in conclusion declares that He who is the sole arbiter of the universe (*vv.* 21-26) is none other than Yahwe, Israel's God (*vv.* 27-31).

prehended the dust of the earth in a measure, and
weighed the mountains in scales, and the hills in a
balance? Who hath directed the spirit of the LORD, 13
or being his counsellor hath taught him? With whom 14
took he counsel, and who instructed him, and taught him
in the path of judgement, and taught him knowledge, and
shewed to him the way of understanding? Behold, the 15
nations are as a drop of a bucket, and are counted as
the small dust of the balance: behold, he taketh up the
isles as a very little thing. And Lebanon is not sufficient 16
to burn, nor the beasts thereof sufficient for a burnt

12-17. The true God has infinite might (*vv.* 11, 12), perfect
wisdom (*vv.* 13, 14), and therefore absolute supremacy over
Man and Nature (*vv.* 15-17).

12. Who...balance: the answer implied by the question is
'None but God.' How immeasurable must be His greatness,
since for the creation of the expanses of the firmament and the
masses of the earth He required only the smallest units of
measurement?

span: the distance between thumb and little finger when the
hand is extended.

comprehended...in a measure: lit. 'weighed out...in a tierce'
(the third part of an *ephah*).

13. Who: here, and in *v.* 14, the answer implied is 'No one.'

spirit of the Lord: generally in the O.T. this phrase denotes
the life-giving power emanating from God. Here it is rather
the equivalent of His intelligence.

14. judgement: or 'right.' The world must be created
and governed equitably.

and...knowledge: omit, as LXX. The clause disturbs the
metre and is redundant.

15. a drop...the balance: a drop hanging from a bucket
or a few grains left in a balance are so small that they make no
appreciable difference to the weight. Even so in comparison
with the Creator all things fade into absolute insignificance.

isles: a word frequently used by II Isaiah. As a rule it
denotes the Mediterranean coastland and adjacent islands, but
in xlii. 15 it is used loosely in the sense of 'habitable land.'

16. Even if the forests of Mt Lebanon and the animals
dwelling on its slopes were offered to God in one vast holocaust,
the sacrifice would not be adequate to His majesty.

17 offering. All the nations are as nothing before him ; they
are counted to him less than nothing, and vanity.

18–20. The idols are nothing but material objects.

18 To whom then will ye liken God? or what likeness will
19 ye compare unto him? The graven image, a workman
melted *it*, and the goldsmith spreadeth it over with gold,
20 and casteth *for it* silver chains. He that is too impover-
ished for *such* an oblation chooseth a tree that will not
rot; he seeketh unto him a cunning workman to set up
a graven image, that shall not be moved.

----

17. less than nothing: or '[formed] of nothing,' i.e. unreal,
without substance.

vanity: lit. 'a waste' (cp. Gen. i. 2, R.V.), i.e. emptiness,
nothing.

18–20. The question at issue has become ridiculous. There
is no comparison between Yahwe and the idols ; for since He
possesses all power, they consequently have none. Manifestly
it would be absurd to try to represent the true God by any
image. Let Israel conclude that the images of the heathen are
impotent fragments of wood and stone, and are wholly con-
temptible. The same topic is dealt with in xliv. 9–20, xlv. 20,
xlvi. 1 f. ; and cp. Acts xvii. 29.

18. God: the word used is a general term, 'Deity,' which
suggests that the argument is addressed to all men and not
merely to the Jews. The gods whom the heathen seek to
portray in their idols do not exist, and the real Deity, after
whom they are ignorantly groping, cannot be depicted by any
image.

19. and casteth...chains: lit. 'and (?) chains of silver a
refiner.' The LXX omits this unintelligible clause. It is
probable that the confusion of the text here and at the beginning
of *v.* 20 has arisen through the misplacement of two verses,
xli. 6, 7 (see notes), which may originally have stood after
the present verse.

20. He that...oblation: again an uncertain clause. Lit. 'he
that is poor as regards a heave-offering' ; but even this quite
unsuitable meaning can hardly be sustained. Of many emendations, the best is Duhm's, 'He who carveth an image....'

21–26. *Know that the Creator of Nature is also the*
ruler of Men.

Have ye not known? have ye not heard? hath it not been 21
told you from the beginning? have ye not understood
from the foundations of the earth? *It is* he that sitteth 22
upon the circle of the earth, and the inhabitants thereof
are as grasshoppers; that stretcheth out the heavens as
a curtain, and spreadeth them out as a tent to dwell in:
that bringeth princes to nothing; he maketh the judges of 23
the earth as vanity. Yea, they have not been planted; 24
yea, they have not been sown; yea, their stock hath not
taken root in the earth: moreover he bloweth upon them,
and they wither, and the whirlwind taketh them away as
stubble. To whom then will ye liken me, that I should 25
be equal *to him*? saith the Holy One. Lift up your eyes 26

21–26. The impotence of the idols having been exposed, the
theme of God's majesty and His supreme control is resumed.

21. Have...known ‖ **have...heard:** better 'Do ye not know?
Do ye not hear?' God does not conceal himself, as Israel
has foolishly imagined (*v.* 27 f.). To the willing mind and the
open ear the truth is always manifest.

from the beginning: the prophet feels that his message is
the realisation of an eternal truth to which all ages have borne
an eloquent though unheeded testimony.

22. he that sitteth: remark the vivid sense of the Divine
activity: He, the real God, sits...stretches...spreads...brings...
makes.

upon (marg. **above**) **the circle:** the 'circle of the earth' is
the line of the vault of the sky, reaching from horizon to
horizon. This vault rests upon the extremities of the world,
which (together with its surrounding ocean) was conceived as
a flat disc. The clouds, stars, and planets were thought of as
situated between the earth and the under-surface, the concave
side, of the arch of heaven: God's dwelling place is above
(upon) the upper side of the vault.

24. Yea...bloweth: read, as marg., 'Scarce are they planted,
scarce are they sown, scarce hath their stock taken root in the
earth, when He bloweth....' So feeble and fleeting is the
power of earthly potentates.

on high, and see who hath created these, that bringeth
out their host by number : he calleth them all by name;
by the greatness of his might, and for that he is strong in
power, not one is lacking.

27–31. *The incomparable God is— Yahwe.*

27 Why sayest thou, O Jacob, and speakest, O Israel, My
way is hid from the LORD, and my judgement is passed
28 away from my God? Hast thou not known? hast thou
not heard ? the everlasting God, the LORD, the Creator
of the ends of the earth, fainteth not, neither is weary ;
29 there is no searching of his understanding. He giveth
power to the faint; and to him that hath no might he
30 increaseth strength. Even the youths shall faint and be
31 weary, and the young men shall utterly fall : but they that
wait upon the LORD shall renew their strength ; they shall

---

26. these : i.e. the stars. If in any mind there still lingers
some fear of the colossal images of the heathen temples, let
the eyes be raised to the infinitude of the starry sky, and let the
mind consider the might of its Creator.

by the...lacking : render 'from Him who is great in might and
strong in power not one is missing.' Every star responds with
unswerving obedience to the Divine roll-call.

27–31. The argument is now clinched. The one God,
glorious and omnipotent, is Yahwe, the God of Israel. What
matter if His ways have been mysterious. Israel must realise
that it has in Him the source of inexhaustible strength and
succour.

27. Yahwe, so Israel has been imagining, has forgotten His
people, and is indifferent to their plight.

my judgement...away : better 'my right (due) is ignored by
my God.' Israel feels that its oppressors have ill-treated it
beyond measure (cp. Zech. i. 15), but its wrongs apparently
roused no resentment in Yahwe.

28. everlasting : God will not therefore grow impatient and
desist from His purpose, although the limited intelligence of
man may fail to perceive His working.

30. youths...young men : i.e. the very perfection of human
strength.

mount up with wings as eagles; they shall run, and not
be weary; they shall walk, and not faint.

xli. *A judgement scene: Yahwe and Israel; the Gentiles
and their so-called Gods.*
1–7. *The signs of the times.*

Keep silence before me, O islands; and let the peoples **41**
renew their strength: let them come near; then let them
speak: let us come near together to judgement. Who 2
hath raised up one from the east, whom he calleth in

---

31. mount up with wings: better, as LXX, 'put forth
pinions.' The thought is not of the renewal of lost strength
but of the acquisition of unexpected powers. Instead of
stumbling wearily along the earth, Israel, if it trust its God,
shall be borne up on the wings of its faith.

xli. The chapter presents a majestic scene in which God
Himself is the central figure and the speaker. Before Him on
the one hand stand the Gentile nations and their deities, gathered
in apparent strength to maintain their claims, and on the other
hand Israel in seeming loneliness and weakness. Addressing
the nations, Yahwe confounds their pretensions to power: they
are on the verge of overthrow at the hands of a new conqueror
whom Yahwe has foreseen, since He it is that has called him
and He that will bring him to complete victory (*vv.* 1–5).
Then turning to Israel, Yahwe owns it as His servant, promising
that it shall receive great glory and be the object of His unfailing
care (*vv.* 8–20). Finally Yahwe challenges the idols to show any
sign of life or of thought. Which of them can thus anticipate
the future? But the idols are silent; the challenge dies away
unanswered (*vv.* 21–28). Verdict accordingly is given: the gods
of the heathen are nought, and their worshippers deluded (*v.* 29).

1–4. The claims on behalf of Yahwe, made generally in
ch. xl., are now brought to the test of contemporary events.

1. renew their strength: the words, which are inappropriate
here, have been copied by mistake from xl. 31. The original
reading was doubtless a verb parallel to that in the first clause,
'keep silence.'

judgement: judicial process, cp. Mal. iii. 5.

2. Who: the answer is of course 'God,' since He alone
can perceive the significance of the new figure in the drama of
history, and can foresee the career of the conqueror whom He
has called into action.

one from the east: the allusion is undoubtedly to Cyrus
(see Introd. p. xiv).

righteousness to his foot? he giveth nations before him,
and maketh him rule over kings; he giveth them as the
3 dust to his sword, as the driven stubble to his bow. He
pursueth them, and passeth on safely; even by a way
4 that he had not gone with his feet. Who hath wrought
and done it, calling the generations from the beginning?
5 I the LORD, the first, and with the last, I am he. The
isles saw, and feared; the ends of the earth trembled:

---

whom...foot: 'whom victory attends at every step.'
According to the Hebrew idea, the litigant who wins his suit
is thereby declared to be 'in the right,' 'righteous,' and here
the ordeal of battle is conceived as a trial of right. Hence
'righteousness' in this passage denotes not a moral quality but
simply the fact of the success of Cyrus in his campaigning, and
is therefore best rendered 'success' or 'victory.' See Introd.
pp. xvi, xxiv.

kings: possibly an allusion to Cyrus' conquest of Astyages,
King of Media, in 549 B.C., and of Croesus of Lydia in 546 B.C.

he giveth...bow: read either 'his sword maketh them like
dust, his bow like driven stubble'; or 'he maketh their sword
as dust, their bow as driven stubble,' i.e. he makes their weapons
utterly impotent to resist the conqueror's advance.

. 3. even...feet: render 'the path with his feet he does not
tread': i.e. so swift is his advance that his feet seem scarcely
to touch the ground.

4. calling...beginning: it is better to take this clause as the
answer to the questions of *vv*. 2–4. Translate 'He that calleth....'

with the last: existent before the dawn of history, Yahwe
remains unceasingly active to the end of time.

I am he: rather 'I am the same.' II Isaiah is fond of this
phrase, which alludes to the explanation of the name 'Yahwe'
as 'I am that I am,' given in Exod. iii. 14 f. He is the
unchanging God.

5. and came: the LXX adds 'together to judgement,' but
the verse, which breaks the connection of Yahwe's speech
(*vv*. 8 ff.) is perhaps a gloss due to the mistaken insertion of
vv. 6, 7—see foll. note.

6, 7. It is highly probable that these verses originally stood
after xl. 19, where they suit the context. In the present position
they are extremely awkward. The only interpretation of the
text as it stands is that the heathen, afraid of the advance of the
conqueror proclaimed by Yahwe, resolve that the best way of
impeding his advance is to construct some new idols.

they drew near, and came. They helped every one his 6
neighbour; and *every one* said to his brother, Be of good
courage. So the carpenter encouraged the goldsmith, 7
and he that smootheth with the hammer him that smiteth
the anvil, saying of the soldering, It is good: and he
fastened it with nails, that it should not be moved.

8-20. *The vindication of Israel.*

But thou, Israel, my servant, Jacob whom I have 8
chosen, the seed of Abraham my friend; thou whom I 9
have taken hold of from the ends of the earth, and called
thee from the corners thereof, and said unto thee, Thou
art my servant, I have chosen thee and not cast thee
away; fear thou not, for I am with thee; be not dis- 10
mayed, for I am thy God: I will strengthen thee; yea,
I will help thee; yea, I will uphold thee with the right

---

6. they: i.e. (in the present context) 'the nations.' If the
verse be read after xl. 19, the reference will be to the various
craftsmen working at the image.

8-20. Turning to Israel, which stands solitary and fearful
(*vv.* 8-10) over against its relentless Gentile oppressors (*v.* 11),
God now announces an amazing change in its fortunes.
Acknowledging it as His beloved servant, He promises a
glorious future of supernatural prosperity (*vv.* 12-20).

8. Israel, my servant: the first occurrence of this title,
which expresses one of the main aspects of II Isaiah's thought.
The term is applied to Israel, in earlier writings, only in
Ezek. xxviii. 25, xxxvii. 25 (for Jer. xxx. 10 f., xlvi. 27 f. are
probably insertions of later date than this prophecy). As the
Servant of Yahwe, Israel has a task to fulfil, of which the
prophet speaks later. Here the thought is of the care and
protection which God will certainly afford to His Servant.

whom I have chosen: cp. John xv. 16: 'Ye did not choose
me, but I chose you....'

Abraham my friend: cp. James ii. 23. Among the Moham-
medans this striking epithet is still applied to Abraham.

9. thou...earth: the reference may be to the call of Abraham
from Mesopotamia (Gen. xii. 1-5); or, less probably, to Israel,
as called forth from Egypt at the time of the Exodus.

10. the right hand...righteousness: i.e. my right hand
which establishes right (or 'success').

11 hand of my righteousness. Behold, all they that are
incensed against thee shall be ashamed and confounded:
they that strive with thee shall be as nothing, and shall
12 perish. Thou shalt seek them, and shalt not find them,
even them that contend with thee: they that war against
13 thee shall be as nothing, and as a thing of nought. For
I the LORD thy God will hold thy right hand, saying unto
14 thee, Fear not; I will help thee. Fear not, thou worm
Jacob, and ye men of Israel; I will help thee, saith the
LORD, and thy redeemer is the Holy One of Israel.
15 Behold, I will make thee a new sharp threshing instrument
having teeth: thou shalt thresh the mountains, and beat
16 them small, and shalt make the hills as chaff. Thou shalt
fan them, and the wind shall carry them away, and the
whirlwind shall scatter them: and thou shalt rejoice in
the LORD, thou shalt glory in the Holy One of Israel.
17 The poor and needy seek water and there is none,

---

14. ye men: a slight change in the Hebrew gives a word
meaning 'small worm.' The emendation is desirable in view of
the parallel clause; cp. Job xxv. 6.

redeemer: Heb. **Gōēl**, a favourite designation of God in
II Isaiah, cp. xliii. 14; xliv. 6, 24; etc. The term is technical
in Hebrew law for that relative whose duty it was to redeem the
person or property of a kinsman from slavery, etc. (Lev. xxv.
47 ff.; Ruth iii. 12; iv. 3 ff.) or to avenge him if murdered
(Num. xxxv. 19 ff.).

15. threshing instrument: the implement in question was in
form a sledge, studded on the underside with knives or jagged
stones ('having teeth'), which was dragged by oxen over the
threshing-floor.

mountains...hills: a fine hyperbole. All opposition shall be
crushed.

16. the wind...away: threshing is followed by winnowing:
the threshed corn was tossed into the air, so that the wind
might blow the light chaff away.

17–20. The glowing promise of the future is adapted to
Israel's immediate necessities. The practical difficulties of
return to Palestine will, the prophet believes, be wonderfully
provided for. The transfigured desert is not to be taken as
merely metaphorical, although doubtless the writer does not
lose sight of a spiritual meaning in his description.

and their tongue faileth for thirst; I the LORD will
answer them, I the God of Israel will not forsake them.
I will open rivers on the bare heights, and fountains in 18
the midst of the valleys: I will make the wilderness a
pool of water, and the dry land springs of water. I will 19
plant in the wilderness the cedar, the acacia tree, and the
myrtle, and the oil tree; I will set in the desert the fir
tree, the pine, and the box tree together: that they may 20
see, and know, and consider, and understand together,
that the hand of the LORD hath done this, and the Holy
One of Israel hath created it.

*21–29.   Yahwe's challenge to the idols: their silence and
His verdict.*

Produce your cause, saith the LORD ; bring forth your 21
strong reasons, saith the King of Jacob. Let them bring 22
them forth, and declare unto us what shall happen:
declare ye the former things, what they be, that we may
consider them, and know the latter end of them; or
shew us things for to come. Declare the things that are 23

---

19.   oil tree : the wild olive, oleaster (as marg.).

20.   they: men in general, but particularly those who scoffed
at Israel's golden hopes.

21–29. The climax of the scene. Israel has been comforted
and gladdened beyond all expectation, whilst the once proud
nations are humiliated and afraid. They have one last hope.
Can their gods save them? To these then God now addresses
an ironical challenge. But the idols stand self-condemned by
their silence: they can neither point to past predictions fulfilled,
nor anticipate the future. There is no power in them, whereas
the conqueror whom Yahwe sustains is resistless. Yahwe's
purpose towards Zion will assuredly be fulfilled.

22.   declare...be: point to predictions of yours, which events
have verified.

and know...come: better, transposing the clauses, ' or let us
hear the things which are to come that we may know their
issue.'

to come hereafter, that we may know that ye are gods:
yea, do good, or do evil, that we may be dismayed, and
24 behold it together.   Behold, ye are of nothing, and your
work of nought: an abomination is he that chooseth you.
25 I have raised up one from the north, and he is come;
from the rising of the sun one that calleth upon my
name: and he shall come upon rulers as upon mortar,
26 and as the potter treadeth clay.   Who hath declared it
from the beginning, that we may know? and beforetime,
that we may say, *He is* righteous? yea, there is none that
declareth, yea, there is none that sheweth, yea, there is
27 none that heareth your words.   *I* first *will say* unto Zion,
Behold, behold them; and I will give to Jerusalem one
28 that bringeth good tidings.   And when I look, there is

---

23.   hereafter: successful prediction suggests the power of
control over future events.   Let this be the test between the
gods and Yahwe.

do...evil: let the idols give any sign, good or bad, of life and
activity.

be dismayed: lit. 'stare,' i.e. be astonished.

24.   of nothing: possibly but not necessarily 'non-existent.'
The meaning is simply that the images and any evil spirits they
represent (if such there be) are absolutely helpless and powerless
to oppose Yahwe.

chooseth you: i.e. worships you.

25.   north...rising of the sun: the first kingdom of Cyrus
lay north-east of Babylonia.

one that...name: recently discovered inscriptions represent
Cyrus as a polytheist.   Perhaps the prophet's expectation is that
Cyrus will eventually recognise that he is Yahwe's agent—render
'shall call' for 'calleth.'   In this way the present passage can
be reconciled with xlv. 4, 'though thou hast not known me.'
Some, however, prefer to make a slight change in the text,
reading 'I have called by name one who shall come....'

come upon: tr. 'tread down.'

26.   righteous: i.e. right.   His prediction has proved correct.

27.   I...will give: the text is faulty.   Read perhaps 'I announce it beforehand to Zion, and give....'   Yahwe's prediction
of Israel's coming deliverance, the good news of xl. 9 ff., contrasts
with the silence of the idols.

**28.   Again the text is uncertain.   The sense seems to be that

no man; even among them there is no counsellor, that,
when I ask of them, can answer a word. Behold, all of 29
them, their works are vanity *and* nought: their molten
images are wind and confusion.

xlii. 1–xliv. 23. *Israel, the Servant of Yahwe.*

xlii. 1–4. *A Song of the Servant* (1).

Behold my servant, whom I uphold; my chosen, in **42**

God nowhere finds evidence of prophetic power, not even
amongst the vaunted idols.

29. them, their : the reference is to the heathen deities
whose impotence has now been proved.

xlii. 1–xliv. 23. In this section the promises of deliverance
and restoration, the leading topics of chs. xl., xli., are continued,
but are set in relation to a central theme—Israel conceived as
the Servant of Yahwe. This designation, already alluded to in
xli. 8, forms the basis of the prophet's exposition of Yahwe's
dealings with His people.

xlii. 1–4. This is the first of four passages, known as the
Servant-songs (viz. xlii. 1–4; xlix. 1–6; l. 4–9; lii. 13–liii. 12), in
which the phrase 'Servant of Yahwe' seems to have a deeper,
more spiritual, significance than when used elsewhere in II Isaiah.
As to the perplexing literary problems raised by these four passages,
see the Introd. pp. xx, xxvi–xxxii.

In the notes it is assumed (1) that the poems are probably an
integral part of II Isaiah's work and not a late insertion; and
(2) that in them, as elsewhere, the Servant personifies the people
of Israel. The prophet, however, regards the nation under
different aspects. Where the title is used in passages other than
these four songs, he thinks chiefly of the historic nation in the
light of its actual experiences; and in those cases Israel, the
Servant, appears to be serving Yahwe rather by a passive
reflection of His will than by an active cooperation in it.
In the Servant-poems, on the other hand, the Servant represents
Israel as it ought to be, a conscious obedient Servant. This
ideal aspect of the nation had its concrete embodiment in the
piety and service of the faithful members of the community,
who, whilst numerically a fraction of Israel, may ideally be
regarded as the whole. Consequently the description of the
Servant in these four passages contains an element of paradox:
he is truly 'Israel,' yet his character far transcends that of the
historic people; he is ideally the whole nation, and yet may
have a duty towards a part, the unbelieving section of the actual
Israel.

1. uphold ; my chosen : the terms are used of Israel in xli. 9, 10,

whom my soul delighteth: I have put my spirit upon
2 him ; he shall bring forth judgement to the Gentiles. He
shall not cry, nor lift up, nor cause his voice to be heard
3 in the street. A bruised reed shall he not break, and the
smoking flax shall he not quench: he shall bring forth
4 judgement in truth. He shall not fail nor be discouraged,
till he have set judgement in the earth ; and the isles
shall wait for his law.

5–9. Yahwe's message of encouragement.

5 Thus saith God the LORD, he that created the heavens,
and stretched them forth; he that spread abroad the

---

xliii. 20, xlv. 4. The LXX reads 'Behold Jacob, my Servant...
Israel, my chosen...'; an explicit identification of the Servant
with the nation.

my spirit: the Servant has a prophet's task and therefore
receives the prophetic endowment.

judgement: collective, as in *vv*. 3, 4, denoting all right
principles and customs. It is equivalent to 'true religion.'

to the Gentiles: in the past Israel has set its hopes on earthly
prosperity. Now, perhaps for the first time, there dawns the
thought of a higher end for national life : the extension of
the blessings of true religion to those in spiritual darkness.
Here is a new commandment—to do good to them that hate
you. Israel is to be Yahwe's prophet to the whole world.

2–4. The Servant's method. The Servant will achieve his
ideal mission by ideal means. The limitations of individual
prophets will be transcended by the ideal prophet. His task
will be accomplished quietly, without the need for self-assertion
(*v*. 2). So profound will be his sympathy and power that he
can succeed in succouring even the feeblest, quickening into new
life their dying possibilities (*v*. 3). Finally, his patience will be
unfailing and will at last crown his efforts with success (*v*. 4).

2.   lift up: *sc.* 'his voice.'

3.   reed...break: the Servant has the supreme gift of an
effective sympathy, which can transform weakness into strength.

smoking flax: better, as marg., 'dimly burning wick.' Instead
of being snuffed out, the flickering light shall again burn steadily.

4.   fail...be discouraged: marg. 'burn dimly...be bruised'
(broken) ; the same words as are used in *v*. 3 of the wick and
the reed.

law: i.e. instruction in the Divine will, not a written code.

earth and that which cometh out of it ; he that giveth
breath unto the people upon it, and spirit to them that
walk therein : I the LORD have called thee in righteous- 6
ness, and will hold thine hand, and will keep thee, and
give thee for a covenant of the people, for a light of the
Gentiles ; to open the blind eyes, to bring out the prisoners 7

5–9. Yahwe now addresses His Servant directly, promising
Divine aid in the achievement of his sacred task (*vv.* 5–7).
These verses are written in the style of II Isaiah, and are
obviously a sequel to *vv.* 1–4, with which they show subtle
points of connection. These facts support the probability that
the Servant-poems are an integral part of the prophecy. Those
scholars who consider the Servant-poems to be a later insertion
have to regard *vv.* 5–7 as linking-verses composed by an
unusually skilful editor. In *vv.* 8–9 we have a concluding
declaration, reaffirming xli. 21–29.

5. spread abroad: render 'made firm,' by beating it out
flat. Note the construction; the verb is made to govern not
only ' the earth ' but also its produce.

6. in righteousness: i.e. in faithful execution of His holy
purpose.

will keep thee: or, in close connection with the foll. clause,
' will form thee ' (so marg.).

I...covenant of the people: a difficult expression, found also
in xlix. 8 (where see note). Having regard to the context, the
best rendering seems to be 'a covenant of people,' where
' covenant ' is equivalent to 'mediator of a covenant' (cp. the
use of 'blessing' in Gen. xii. 2) and 'people' means 'humanity'
in general. The sense would be that God appoints the Servant
(Israel) to mediate unto all mankind a covenant relationship with
Himself. This interpretation agrees with the fact that in *vv.* 1–4
the Servant's task relates to humanity (the Gentiles), and it also
has the merit of preserving the parallel with the following
appositional clause, in which the Servant is described as a
' light ' in the sense that he is a bringer of light. An objection,
but not a fatal one, is that the word translated ' people ' rarely
means 'mankind'; see, however, xl. 7, xlii. 5.

7. to open...to bring: the Heb. leaves it ambiguous whether
the subj. of the verbs is Yahwe or the Servant. The same
ambiguity occurs in xlix. 8. If the Servant be the subject, the
metaphors of *v.* 9 ('dungeon,' 'prison-house') are to be interpreted generally as terms for spiritual ignorance. If Yahwe,
then the reference *may* be specifically to deliverance from exile :
God must first set free His people preliminary to their work

E.   2

from the dungeon, and them that sit in darkness out of
8 the prison house.   I am the LORD ; that is my name :
and my glory will I not give to another, neither my praise
9 unto graven images.   Behold, the former things are come
to pass, and new things do I declare : before they spring
forth I tell you of them.

10–13.   A Psalm: the praise of Yahwe.

10   Sing unto the LORD a new song, and his praise from
the end of the earth ; ye that go down to the sea, and all
11 that is therein, the isles, and the inhabitants thereof.   Let
the wilderness and the cities thereof lift up *their voice*,
the villages that Kedar doth inhabit ; let the inhabitants
of Sela sing, let them shout from the top of the mountains.
12 Let them give glory unto the LORD, and declare his
13 praise in the islands.   The LORD shall go forth as a

---

as His Servant among the Gentiles.   In this case we should
translate 'by opening...by bringing out....'

9. former things : i.e. events which had been foretold in
prophecies.   Precisely what predictions are alluded to is uncertain, perhaps some concerning the rise and advance of Cyrus.
The 'new things' now predicted are the startling promises set
forth in *vv.* 14–17 (see note *v.* 14), or, more generally, the
coming exaltation of Israel and the work of the Servant.

10–13.   A hymn claiming universal praise for Yahwe and
anticipating a wondrous display of His power.

10. new song : so also in many Psalms, e.g. xl. 3, xcvi. 1,
xcviii. 1 ; and Rev. xiv. 3.   This 'new song' is perhaps a later
addition, suggested by the phrase 'new things' in *v.* 9.

ye that...therein : render 'let the sea roar and the fulness
thereof,' cp. Ps. xcvi. 11.

11. cities thereof : i.e. permanent settlements in the oases,
such as Tadmor.

Kedar : an Arab tribe to the east of Palestine, partly
nomadic (Ps. cxx. 5), partly village-dwellers (so here).

inhabitants of Sela : Sela is possibly Petra, some fifty miles
south of the Dead Sea ; but an equally sound translation is
simply 'rock-dwellers.'

13.   The ground for rejoicing is that Yahwe Himself goes
out to battle against His foes.

mighty man ; he shall stir up jealousy like a man of war :
he shall cry, yea, he shall shout aloud ; he shall do
mightily against his enemies.

14–17. *Yahwe will exert His might.*

I have long time holden my peace ; I have been still, and 14
refrained myself : *now* will I cry out like a travailing
woman ; I will gasp and pant together. I will make 15
waste mountains and hills, and dry up all their herbs ;
and I will make the rivers islands, and will dry up the
pools. And I will bring the blind by a way that they 16
know not ; in paths that they know not will I lead them :
I will make darkness light before them, and crooked
places straight. These things will I do, and I will not
forsake them. They shall be turned back, they shall be 17
greatly ashamed, that trust in graven images, that say
unto molten images, Ye are our gods.

---

jealousy : better 'ardour,' i.e. battle-fever.

cry : i.e. raise the battle-shout.

14–17. These verses are the continuation of Yahwe's speech
in *vv.* 1–9, for their metrical form is that of *vv.* 1–9, differing
from that of *vv.* 10–13, and the 'new things which God is about
to declare' (*v.* 9) are the astonishing promises given in *vv.* 15, 16.

15. Contrast the effects of God's mercy as set forth in xli. 18 ff.

islands : see xl. 15, note.

16. A verse of gracious assurance of help. The reference
may be to the return of the exiles ('the blind') through the
trackless desert ('darkness'), or, more generally, to the deliverance of those ignorant of Yahwe from their spiritual darkness.
But in either case the abrupt introduction of such a promise
between the menaces of *vv.* 14, 15 and 17 is strange, and the
verse is perhaps an addition.

straight : better 'a plain.'

not forsake them : 'not leave them undone.'

18–25. From the ideal picture of *vv.* 1–4, the prophet turns
to face present realities. How great the contrast between the
ideal Israel and the real ! Considering its opportunities, Israel
actually appears more blind than the heathen whom it should
enlighten (*vv.* 18–21). Above all, it has failed to comprehend
the inner significance of its fall and exile (*vv.* 22–25).

18-25. The Spiritual Poverty of Yahwe's Servant.

18 Hear, ye deaf; and look, ye blind, that ye may see.
19 Who is blind, but my servant? or deaf, as my messenger
that I send? who is blind as he that is at peace *with me*,
20 and blind as the LORD's servant? Thou seest many
things, but thou observest not; his ears are open, but he
21 heareth not. It pleased the LORD, for his righteousness'
22 sake, to magnify the law, and make it honourable. But
this is a people robbed and spoiled; they are all of them
snared in holes, and they are hid in prison houses: they
are for a prey, and none delivereth; for a spoil, and none
23 saith, Restore. Who is there among you that will give
ear to this? that will hearken and hear for the time to
24 come? Who gave Jacob for a spoil, and Israel to the

---

18. Whether the appeal is addressed to all who lack spiritual
illumination, or simply to such Israelites as are 'deaf' and
'blind,' is uncertain.

that ye may see: at last let them learn to perceive the true
meaning of their disaster in the light of the Divine purpose.

19. he that is at peace: the precise meaning is doubtful.
Perhaps 'he that is requited' (*i.e.* a paid servant), or less probably
'the devoted one.'

20. observest not: it is the people's own fault that they
have failed to read the meaning of their history, and the teaching
of their prophets.

21. righteousness: God's fidelity in carrying out His
purposes, as in *v.* 6.

magnify the law: i.e. to glorify the body of truth ('instruction' or 'revelation,' cp. *v.* 4), which proceeds from Him, by
making it effective amongst all nations.

22. But here is an enigma. How is the pitiable, apparently
hopeless, plight of Israel, Yahwe's agent, to be reconciled with
the assertion of His power and immutable purpose?

23. Who will listen to the solution of this dark problem, and
realise the eternal principle wherein lies both the explanation of
present misery and the hope of future restoration?

24. Who...spoil. Their national overthrow formed the
supreme religious difficulty for the Jews. According to the
ideas of the period it betokened either that God had finally
abandoned His people, or else that the gods of the conqueror

robbers? did not the LORD? he against whom we have
sinned, and in whose ways they would not walk, neither
were they obedient unto his law. Therefore he poured 25
upon him the fury of his anger, and the strength of battle;
and it set him on fire round about, yet he knew not ; and
it burned him, yet he laid it not to heart.

xliii. 1–7. *The Redemption of Israel.*

But now thus saith the LORD that created thee, O **43**
Jacob, and he that formed thee, O Israel : Fear not, for
I have redeemed thee ; I have called thee by thy name,
thou art mine. When thou passest through the waters, I **2**
will be with thee; and through the rivers, they shall not
overflow thee: when thou walkest through the fire, thou
shalt not be burned; neither shall the flame kindle upon
thee. For I am the LORD thy God, the Holy One of 3
Israel, thy saviour ; I have given Egypt as thy ransom,

---

were more powerful than He. The prophet would force the
doubters to face the problem again. There is another possibility ——

did not the Lord : let Israel realise that the disaster took
place not against but in accordance with the will of God, and
hope will be once more reasonable. But, if so, what was the
motive for His action?

we have sinned: the prophet interprets the suffering as the
moral discipline of a righteous God.

xliii. 1–7. These verses continue and conclude the preceding
section. The prophet has more to give than the negative
consolation of showing that Israel's humiliation was consistent
with Yahwe's love. Now, he declares, the hidden but unabated
tenderness of Yahwe will be poured forth in blessings upon His
chastened people.

1. I have redeemed...called : better 'I will surely redeem...
call.' The Hebrew expresses the idea that the act, though
future, is certain of fulfilment.

by thy name : i.e. with special tenderness singling out Israel
from among the nations.

2. waters...rivers...fire : natural images for extreme peril.

3. Egypt as thy ransom : there will be a renewal of the
age-long struggle between the empires of the North and of the

4 Ethiopia and Seba for thee. Since thou hast been precious
in my sight, *and* honourable, and I have loved thee;
therefore will I give men for thee, and peoples for thy
5 life. Fear not; for I am with thee: I will bring thy seed
6 from the east, and gather thee from the west; I will say
to the north, Give up; and to the south, Keep not back;
bring my sons from far, and my daughters from the end
7 of the earth; every one that is called by my name, and
whom I have created for my glory; I have formed him;
yea, I have made him.

8–13. Israel, Yahwe's Witness.

8 Bring forth the blind people that have eyes, and the

South. Yahwe, Israel's deliverer ('Saviour,' as in *v.* 11,
xlv. 15, 21, xlix. 26), will grant victory to the North, permitting
Cyrus to subdue Egypt and its neighbouring territories as a
reward for his liberation of Israel. In point of fact the Persians
did succeed in conquering Egypt, not however in the days of
Cyrus, but during the reign of his son Cambyses. The sentiment
of the verse need not be construed as expressing hostility or
indifference to the fate of the Gentile peoples. It is simply a
rhetorical assertion that God's love for his people will place
no limits on his willingness to secure their deliverance. The
details of the picture should not be pressed and then regarded
as inconsistent with the tone of genuinely universal sympathy,
which forms so striking a feature of II Isaiah's religious standpoint.

Seba: perhaps Meroe on the Nile, near the modern
Khartoum.

4. men: Israel's ransom is paid not in gold but in whole
nations.

5, 6. east...west...north...south. We are apt to exaggerate
the relative importance of the Babylonian exiles. Recent dis-
coveries make it certain that the Jewish communities in Egypt
even at this date were not only flourishing but also patriotic in
sentiment and loyal in their adhesion to the worship of Yahwe.
The prophet looks for an ingathering of the whole Dispersion,
cp. xlix. 12.

8–13. Again, as in ch. xli., a judgment scene. Yahwe
challenges the nations to produce evidence of foreknowledge.
They stand silent, whilst Israel is declared to be His witness,
the proof that He alone is the true God.

8. Bring forth: i.e. before the judgment throne.

deaf that have ears.   Let all the nations be gathered 9
together, and let the peoples be assembled: who among
them can declare this, and shew us former things? let
them bring their witnesses, that they may be justified:
or let them hear, and say, It is truth.   Ye are my wit- 10
nesses, saith the LORD, and my servant whom I have
chosen: that ye may know and believe me, and understand that I am he; before me there was no God formed,
neither shall there be after me.   I, even I, am the LORD; 11
and beside me there is no saviour.   I have declared, and 12
I have saved, and I have shewed, and there was no
strange *god* among you: therefore ye are my witnesses,
saith the LORD, and I am God.   Yea, since the day was 13

---

blind...eyes...deaf...ears: Israel has witnessed the verifica-
tion of predictions uttered by Yahwe's prophets in bygone
years.   It can at any rate testify to the facts it has seen and
heard, even if it has been unaware of their full significance.

9. Let...assembled: better 'all the nations are gathered
together, and the peoples are assembled.'

can declare this: i.e. the redemption of Israel, which God
alone is able to foretell.

former things: or, if they should venture on so strange a
declaration, then let them quote in confirmation past predictions
which have come true.

let them hear: i.e. let the witnesses confirm the truth of any
allegations which the idols may put forth.

10.   The gods of the nations have no assertions to make, no
witnesses to put forward.   But Yahwe's witness is at hand: even
Israel, his servant-people.

that ye may know: in the act of bearing testimony to the
simple facts Israel will learn their inner meaning.

12. and there was no strange (god) among you: *sc.* who
'declared and saved and shewed,' as Yahwe.   The implication
is that Yahwe alone is real, and that Israel's salvation has been
effected by Him and by Him alone.

therefore: render simply 'and.'

13. since the day was: rather, as marg., 'from this day
forth': i.e. the day of redemption marks a new epoch in Yahwe's
self-manifestation.

I am he; and there is none that can deliver out of my hand: I will work, and who shall let it?

14-21. *The Fall of Babylon, and the new Exodus.*

14   Thus saith the LORD, your redeemer, the Holy One of Israel: For your sake I have sent to Babylon, and I will bring down all of them as fugitives, even the Chaldeans,
15 in the ships of their rejoicing. I am the LORD, your
16 Holy One, the Creator of Israel, your King. Thus saith the LORD, which maketh a way in the sea, and a path in
17 the mighty waters; which bringeth forth the chariot and horse, the army and the power; they lie down together, they shall not rise; they are extinct, they are quenched
18 as flax: Remember ye not the former things, neither con-
19 sider the things of old. Behold, I will do a new thing; now shall it spring forth; shall ye not know it? I will even make a way in the wilderness, and rivers in the

---

let it: i.e. 'reverse' (as marg.), or 'prevent it'; cp. Exod. v. 4 (A.V.).

14-21. The Exodus from Egypt, the great landmark of history for Israel, will not need to be remembered by reason of the glories of the impending new deliverance.

14. I have sent: *sc.* the Persian army. The perfect tense here expresses certainty, i.e. 'I shall assuredly send.'

Babylon: the first explicit reference to Babylon in the prophecy.

I will...rejoicing: the text is probably at fault, but no satisfactory correction has been suggested. As it stands, the meaning must be that, when Cyrus advances on the city, the Babylonians will seek to escape down the river on board the galleys of which they boasted.

16-18. God's promise (*vv.* 18 ff.) is introduced by recalling (*vv.* 16, 17) the thought of the saving power displayed by Him at the Exodus from Egypt.

17. bringeth forth: *sc.* to their destruction.

quenched as flax: render 'extinguished like a wick'; cp. xlii. 3.

18. Remember ye not: not, of course, a command to forget the mercies of the past: only that the new deliverance is to replace the Exodus from Egypt as Israel's most cherished memory.

19. shall ye...it: better 'do ye not perceive it?'

desert. The beasts of the field shall honour me, the 20
jackals and the ostriches: because I give waters in the
wilderness, and rivers in the desert, to give drink to
my people, my chosen: the people which I formed for 21
myself, that they might set forth my praise.

*22–25. Israel's past Ingratitude: Yahwe's Mercy
and Discipline.*

Yet thou hast not called upon me, O Jacob; but thou hast 22
been weary of me, O Israel. Thou hast not brought me 23
the small cattle of thy burnt offerings; neither hast thou
honoured me with thy sacrifices. I have not made thee
to serve with offerings, nor wearied thee with frankincense.
Thou hast bought me no sweet cane with money, neither 24
hast thou filled me with the fat of thy sacrifices: but thou
hast made me to serve with thy sins, thou hast wearied
me with thine iniquities.

---

20. The joy of the creatures, whose thirst has been satisfied,
will be a real praise to Him who has so marvellously supplied
their needs. The thought would seem far less strange to the
ancient than to the modern mind; cp. Is. xi. 6–9.

to my people: refreshing streams were created not for the
desert animals, but for Israel. Let not Israel fail to render thanks.

22–28. Again the prophet turns from the ideal to the real.
Instead of thankful praise, Israel has displayed only determined
neglect of its God and transgression of His law. Nevertheless
Yahwe has remained the God who is 'slow to anger and
plenteous in mercy.'

22. but...of me: read 'neither hast (or 'much less hast')
thou wearied thyself about me.'

23, 24. Israel has neglected the most ordinary outward acts of
reverence towards its God; and the shame of this omission is in no
wise lessened by the fact that Yahwe, in contrast to the heathen
gods, has laid no stress on ritual worship (*v.* 23). But, whereas He
has been so unexacting in this matter, Israel by its immoralities
has taxed to the uttermost the forbearance of His love (*v.* 24).

24. sweet cane: a scented reed, frequently mentioned in Babylonian records as an ingredient of sacrifices. Cp. Exod. xxx. 23.

but thou...iniquities: how great the contrast! Whereas
Israel has borne no burden for Yahwe's honour—it has not paid
Him even the commonplaces of ordinary ritual worship—Yahwe
has endured the pain and burden of its persistent sinfulness.

xliii. 25-xliv. 5.   *The Graciousness of God.*

25 I, even I, am he that blotteth out thy transgressions for
26 mine own sake; and I will not remember thy sins.   Put
me in remembrance; let us plead together: set thou forth
27 *thy cause*, that thou mayest be justified.   Thy first father
sinned, and thine interpreters have transgressed against
28 me.   Therefore I will profane the princes of the sanctuary,
and I will make Jacob a curse, and Israel a reviling.
44 Yet now hear, O Jacob my servant; and Israel, whom I
2 have chosen: thus saith the LORD that made thee, and
formed thee from the womb, who will help thee: Fear

---

25.   A verse of perfect tenderness, which reveals the tragedy
of all sin, not merely that of ancient Israel.   The pathos of the
situation is not that Israel has defied power, but that it has
despised love, a love which forgave and will still forgive.

for mine own sake: what is the ultimate ground of the
forgiveness of sin?   Not any merit which the people can plead
(*v.* 26), but God's own nature of unchanging love, which
eternally constrains Him to 'bring out the prisoners from the
dungeon,' even though the deliverance can be accomplished
only by first letting Israel go into exile—and Christ to His
Cross.

26.   If there be any merit which Yahwe has overlooked, let
Israel plead its case.   Its silence condemns it.

27. first father: not Adam nor Abraham, but Jacob (Israel)
is meant, whose name was bestowed on the nation as a whole.

interpreters: i.e. the prophets.   We must remember that
the true prophets were few and the false many.   Cp. Jer. xxiii.
11 ff.; 1 Kings xxii. 10 ff.   If patriarch and prophet have
sinned, how much more the mass of the people!

28.   Translate 'Therefore I had to profane the consecrated
leaders (i.e. both priests and kings), and to give up Jacob to the
ban and Israel to revilings.'

xliv. 1-5.   The gracious utterance of Yahwe concludes with
the promise of a glorious future.   He has declared his unfailing
lovingkindness despite Israel's ingratitude, and has shown that
its humiliations are the necessary consequence of its sin against
a holy God.   But the present state of misery is almost ended
(cp. xlii. 25-xliii. 1), for the mercy of Yahwe is about to descend
in such blessings on Israel that even strangers will be eager to
join themselves to the people of Yahwe.

not, O Jacob my servant; and thou, Jeshurun, whom I
have chosen.   For I will pour water upon him that is 3
thirsty, and streams upon the dry ground: I will pour my
spirit upon thy seed, and my blessing upon thine offspring: and they shall spring up among the grass, as 4
willows by the watercourses.   One shall say, I am the 5
LORD'S; and another shall call *himself* by the name of
Jacob; and another shall subscribe with his hand unto
the LORD, and surname *himself* by the name of Israel.

6-23. *A contrast: the eternal God and the man-made idols.*

Thus saith the LORD, the King of Israel, and his 6
redeemer the LORD of hosts: I am the first, and I am
the last; and beside me there is no God.   And who, as I, 7

---

2.   Jeshurun: a rare synonym for Israel (elsewhere only
Deut. xxxii. 15, xxxiii. 5, 26).   The word is connected with an
adj. 'Jashar' ('upright')—cp. Josh. x. 13, 'the book of Jashar.'
The title is therefore an honourable one, and perhaps is selected
as an antithesis to the stigma implied in the name Jacob
('supplanter').

4.   among the grass: read, with LXX, 'as grass among
the waters,' i.e. grass growing in meadows full of moisture.

5.   One...another: i.e. individual foreign proselytes shall
covet the privileges of belonging to Israel, cp. xiv. 1.   The
prophet has seen the ideal of a humanity united in the bond of
religious brotherhood.

subscribe...Lord: render 'inscribe "to Yahwe" upon his
hand,' in token of self-dedication.   We may compare the
practices of branding slaves with their owner's name, or the
tattooing of tribal or sacred marks on the body; see Ez. ix. 4;
Lev. xix. 28; Gal. vi. 17.

surname...Israel: the proselyte shall count it an honour to
add the designation 'Israelite' to his name.

6-23.   A reiteration of the leading themes of the previous
chapters.   (*a*) *vv.* 6-8.   Yahwe is the one eternal God.   (*b*) 9-20.
The worship of idols is manifestly absurd.   (*c*) Mindful of the
mercy of its God, let Israel render Him joyful thanks.

6.   King of Israel: cp. xli. 21.

first, and...last: 'grander than even His preeminence in space
is His preeminence in time' (Duhm).   Cp. xlviii. 12; Rev. i. 8,
xxii. 13.

shall call, and shall declare it, and set it in order for me,
since I appointed the ancient people? and the things that
are coming, and that shall come to pass, let them declare.
8 Fear ye not, neither be afraid : have I not declared unto
thee of old, and shewed it? and ye are my witnesses. Is
there a God beside me? yea, there is no Rock; I know
9 not any. They that fashion a graven image are all of
them vanity; and their delectable things shall not profit :
and their own witnesses see not, nor know; that they may
10 be ashamed. Who hath fashioned a god, or molten
11 a graven image that is profitable for nothing? Behold,
all his fellows shall be ashamed; and the workmen, they

---

7. Following the LXX, read 'And who is like Me? Let
him stand forth and speak out and declare it and set it in order
for Me. Who hath announced from of old future things? And
that which shall come to pass let them declare unto us': an
appeal to the witness of successful prediction, cp. xli. 22 ff.;
xliii. 9–12.

8. **Rock :** as a great rock in the desert is the only place of
protection from the burning heat of the sands, so in Yahwe alone
can refuge be found: cp. Deut. xxxii. 4 ff.

9–20. These verses are written in prose, whereas *vv.* 6–8,
21 ff. are in metre. It is therefore probable that the passage is
a later insertion. As far as the subject-matter is concerned, it is
of course a perfectly suitable sequel to *vv.* 6–8: cp. xl. 18–20
following 12–17.

9. delectable things : i.e. favourite images.

their own witnesses : those who worship the idols (cp. xliii. 8)
are without true insight and wisdom.

that...ashamed : the shame which is the inevitable result of
their folly is sarcastically stated as if it was the aim and object
of their deliberate blind unintelligence. This peculiar Hebraic
idiom is important for the interpretation of passages in the New
as well as the Old Testament, cp. Hos. viii. 4; Matt. xiii. 13–15
(quoting Is. vi. 9, 10).

10. Who...nothing? A rhetorical question, expecting a
negative answer. Better, however, is the rendering 'Whoso
hath fashioned a god hath molten a useless image.'

11. all his fellows : i.e. his fellow-worshippers. An interesting emendation for the clause 'Behold...men' has been
suggested : 'Behold, all his (the idol-maker's) spells are put to
shame, and the enchantments are of man (mere human devices).'

are of men: let them all be gathered together, let them
stand up; they shall fear, they shall be ashamed together.
The smith *maketh* an axe, and worketh in the coals, and 12
fashioneth it with hammers, and worketh it with his
strong arm: yea, he· is hungry, and his strength faileth;
he drinketh no water, and is faint. The carpenter 13
stretcheth out a line; he marketh it out with a pencil;
he shapeth it with planes, and he marketh it out with the
compasses, and shapeth it after the figure of a man,
according to the beauty of a man, to dwell in the house.
He heweth him down cedars, and taketh the holm tree 14
and the oak, and strengtheneth for himself one among
the trees of the forest: he planteth a fir tree, and the rain
doth nourish it. Then shall it be for a man to burn; and 15
he taketh thereof, and warmeth himself; yea, he kindleth
it, and baketh bread: yea, he maketh a god, and worshippeth it; he maketh it a graven image, and falleth
down thereto. He burneth part thereof in the fire; with 16
part thereof he eateth flesh; he roasteth roast, and is

If this be correct, the allusion is to incantations used with the
intention of transforming the image into a fetish, the abode of
a spirit.

12–17. The ludicrous details of manufacturing the idols.

12. The smith...coals: the text is corrupt: render perhaps
'the blacksmith worketh with the coals.'

it: the image, hammered into shape while the molten metal
is still soft.

his strength faileth: cp. xl. 31, the contrast may be present
to the writer's mind.

13. The carpenter: a worker in wood carefully fashions an
image of human shape for erection in some shrine ('to dwell in
the house').

14–20. Still clearer will seem the infatuation of the idolater
if we trace the manufacture of a wooden image from its origin.

14. he planteth...it: the LXX has a fine variant, 'which
God planted and the rain nourished.'

15, 16. When the tree is felled, it is not even consecrated as
a whole to the manufacture of the image: part supplies the
idolater with common fuel for hearth or oven, the remainder
becomes his god.

satisfied : yea, he warmeth himself, and saith, Aha, I am
17 warm, I have seen the fire : and the residue thereof he
maketh a god, even his graven image : he falleth down
unto it and worshippeth, and prayeth unto it, and saith,
18 Deliver me; for thou art my god. They know not,
neither do they consider : for he hath shut their eyes,
that they cannot see ; and their hearts, that they cannot
19 understand. And none calleth to mind, neither is there
knowledge nor understanding to say, I have burned part
of it in the fire ; yea, also I have baked bread upon the
coals thereof; I have roasted flesh and eaten it : and
shall I make the residue thereof an abomination ? shall
20 I fall down to the stock of a tree ? He feedeth on ashes :
a deceived heart hath turned him aside, that he cannot
deliver his soul, nor say, Is there not a lie in my right
hand ?
21 Remember these things, O Jacob; and Israel, for thou
art my servant : I have formed thee ; thou art my servant :
22 O Israel, thou shalt not be forgotten of me. I have
blotted out, as a thick cloud, thy transgressions, and, as
a cloud, thy sins : return unto me ; for I have redeemed
23 thee. Sing, O ye heavens, for the LORD hath done it;

---

18. he hath shut...eyes : lit. 'their eyes are besmeared.'
Only the absence of spiritual and intellectual insight can account
for such abject folly as has just been described.

19. calleth to mind : cp. xlvi. 8. If they would but reflect,
such conduct would surely become impossible.

abomination : a contemptuous expression for an idol. In
xlix. 24 it is applied to the idolater himself.

20. He feedeth on ashes : to 'feed on ashes' may mean
that the idolater sets his hopes on a thing which fire can reduce
to ashes, or it may be a proverbial phrase for resting content
with what is essentially base or useless. A better rendering is
'He who feeds on ashes—a deceived heart....'

a lie...hand : i.e. that he is relying on a fraud.

21-23. Remembering these facts and its relation to the true
God, let Israel rejoice in His mercy.

23. A paean of praise, marking the end of the section.

shout, ye lower parts of the earth; break forth into
singing, ye mountains, O forest, and every tree therein :
for the LORD hath redeemed Jacob, and will glorify himself in Israel.

xliv. 24-xlv. 25. *The restoration of Israel through
Cyrus, the Lord's anointed.*

xliv. 24-xlv. 8. *The mission of Cyrus.*

Thus saith the LORD, thy redeemer, and he that formed 24
thee from the womb : I am the LORD, that maketh all
things; that stretcheth forth the heavens alone ; that
spreadeth abroad the earth; who is with me? that frus- 25
trateth the tokens of the liars, and maketh diviners mad ;
that turneth wise men backward, and maketh their knowledge foolish : that confirmeth the word of his servant, 26
and performeth the counsel of his messengers ; that saith
of Jerusalem, She shall be inhabited; and of the cities of

---

lower parts : the abysses of earth, reaching down to Sheol
(Ps. lxiii. 9).
xliv. 24-xlv. 25. As the proclamation of monotheism culmi-
nated in the revelation that the omnipotent God is none other
than Yahwe (xl. 27-31), so now the indefinite promises of redemption sharpen into a clear assertion in the sphere of contemporary events: the deliverer is at hand, is a known historic
personality, is Cyrus.
24-28. God, addressing Israel, proclaims His nature and
His immediate purpose, and reveals the name of the appointed
deliverer, Cyrus.
24. who is with me ? i.e. who helped me in the work of
creation? Cp. xl. 13.
25. tokens of the liars : or 'omens of the babblers'—the arts
of divination for which Babylonia was proverbially famous,
cp. xlvii. 9 ff.; Horace, *Odes* I. xi. 2, 3.
26. servant : read, as LXX, 'servants,' parallel to 'messengers.' Both words refer to the true prophets of Israel whose
word God confirms, in sharp contrast to the magicians whose
arts He confounds.
Jerusalem : at last the explicit affirmation of that for which
Israel has so passionately longed.

Judah, They shall be built, and I will raise up the waste
27 places thereof: that saith to the deep, Be dry, and I will
28 dry up thy rivers: that saith of Cyrus, *He is* my shepherd,
and shall perform all my pleasure: even saying of
Jerusalem, She shall be built; and to the temple, Thy
foundation shall be laid.

45   Thus saith the LORD to his anointed, to Cyrus, whose
right hand I have holden, to subdue nations before him,

---

of the cities...built: the clause disturbs the metre, and is
therefore to be omitted as a gloss.

27. the deep: possibly with thought of the ancient deliverance at the Red Sea, cp. xliii. 16. The word is, of course,
symbolic here of all opposition to Israel's restoration.

28. Cyrus: we gather that as yet few, if any, had sur-
mised that Cyrus might one day conquer Babylon. Even if he
did, what would a change of ruler matter to scattered Israel?
The prophet saw further. Behind Cyrus, he beheld the hand
of Israel's Redeemer, guiding his steps and making his advance
resistless.

shepherd: i.e. ruler. Some prefer to read 'my friend,'
a very slight change in the Hebrew.

my pleasure: i.e. my purpose. The end of the victories
which Yahwe grants to Cyrus will be the accomplishment of
Yahwe's will.

even saying: the subject is Cyrus, but the text is probably
incorrect. The LXX has 'that saith,' making Yahwe the
subject as in the previous verses. In that case, however, the
clause seems redundant after *v.* 26, and is open to suspicion as a
later addition.

xlv. 1-7. Yahwe, now addressing Cyrus, summons him to
accomplish the Divine purpose with the assurance of Divine
support.

1. to his anointed: in later times the term acquired the
meaning 'Messiah,' but in the O.T. it is applied only to the
Kings and (in Ps. cv. 15) to the Patriarchs. In the present
passage alone is the title used of a foreign monarch, but Cyrus
may justly receive it on account of his unique relationship to
Israel.

to Cyrus: the metrical form of the verse strongly suggests
that 'to Cyrus' is an interpretative gloss, although of course the
interpretation may be quite correct. Other means of rectifying
the metre are possible.

and I will loose the loins of kings ; to open the doors
before him, and the gates shall not be shut ; I will go 2
before thee, and make the rugged places plain : I will
break in pieces the doors of brass, and cut in sunder the
bars of iron : and I will give thee the treasures of dark- 3
ness, and hidden riches of secret places, that thou mayest
know that I am the LORD, which call thee by thy name,
even the God of Israel. For Jacob my servant's sake, 4
and Israel my chosen, I have called thee by thy name :
I have surnamed thee, though thou hast not known me.
I am the LORD, and there is none else ; beside me there 5
is no God : I will gird thee, though thou hast not known
me : that they may know from the rising of the sun, and 6
from the west, that there is none beside me : I am the
LORD, and there is none else.   I form the light, and 7

---

loose the loins : i.e. render weak and helpless.   Contrast 'I
girded thee,' *v.* 5.
    3. of darkness : i.e. concealed in the most secret places.
Probably the prophet is thinking of the fabulous treasures of
Croesus, King of Lydia, whose capital, Sardis, had already been
captured by Cyrus.   The wealth of Babylon, the richest city of
the world, will also become his possession.
    that thou...Lord : cp. xli. 25.   The prophet's expectation that
Cyrus would eventually see in Yahwe the cause of his victories
and acknowledge Him as the one true God was not realised.
From the language of his inscriptions, Cyrus seems to have
remained a polytheist, tolerant and impartial towards the various
gods of his subject-nations.   Whether his attitude was determined
by conviction or simply by political motives cannot be settled.
    4. For Jacob...sake : in the prophet's thought the achieve-
ment of Yahwe's ultimate purpose—recognition by all men of
His sovereignty and sole Divinity (*vv.* 5, 6)—and the vindication
of Israel are inseparably connected.   Through His dealings
with Israel, the ultimate object will be attained; such is the
method of the Divine working.
    surnamed thee : with honourable titles, such as 'My shep-
herd,' 'My anointed.'
    5. though...me : see the note to xli. 25.
    6. they : all men.

E.   3

create darkness ; I make peace, and create evil ; I am
the LORD, that doeth all these things.

8   Drop down, ye heavens, from above, and. let the skies
pour down righteousness : let the earth open, that they
may bring forth salvation, and let her cause righteousness
to spring up together ; I the LORD have created it.

9-13.   Yahwe's manner of working must not be questioned.

9   Woe unto him that striveth with his Maker ! a potsherd
among the potsherds of the earth !   Shall the clay say to
him that fashioneth it, What makest thou ? or thy work,
10 He hath no hands ?   Woe unto him that saith unto a

---

7.   peace : 'well-being,' 'good fortune.'

I...create evil : cp. xli. 23, where the idols are called upon
'to do good or do evil,' if they can. The present verse is an
emphatic declaration that nothing happens without the knowledge and will of God, cp. Am. iii. 6; and 'evil' signifies physical
evil, suffering, catastrophes. It is quite wrong to suppose that the
prophet has in mind the question of the origin of moral evil:
that in the O.T. is regarded as proceeding from the will of man,
whilst physical evil is sent by God as a punishment for sin. Nor
is it likely that there is here any thought of the dualism of
Zoroastrianism (probably the actual religion of Cyrus) with its
doctrine of the struggle between Ahuramazda, god of light and
goodness, and Ahriman, god of darkness and evil.

8. A lyrical interlude, as in xlii. 10-14, xliv. 23, expressing
the joy of all creation at the universal acknowledgment of the
true religion.

drop down : *sc.* 'righteousness': the verb is active.

righteousness : rather 'right,' i.e. the Divine principle, justice.
Later in the verse the word denotes the same quality as displayed
in the relationships of human society.

that they...salvation : render 'and let salvation and [...]
spring forth': a noun has dropped out of the text after 'salvation.'

her : i.e. the earth, on which God's blessings have been poured
forth like fructifying rain.

9-13. These verses appear to be directed against a section of
the people who have displayed active resentment of the strange
manner in which God is said to be about to effect their deliverance. Compare the tone of xl. 27, li. 13, where, however,
the prophet has to rebuke merely timid incredulity.

9.   a potsherd...earth : God is the potter, man the clay.

or...hands : read 'or his work, Thou hast no hands.'

father, What begettest thou? or to a woman, With what
travailest thou? Thus saith the LORD, the Holy One 11
of Israel, and his Maker: Ask me of the things that are
to come ; concerning my sons, and concerning the work
of my hands, command ye me. I have made the earth, 12
and created man upon it : I, even my hands, have
stretched out the heavens, and all their host have I
commanded. I have raised him up in righteousness, and 13
I will make straight all his ways : he shall build my city,
and he shall let my exiles go free, not for price nor reward,
saith the LORD of hosts.

14–17.   *The nations of Africa pay homage to Yahwe
and to Israel.*

Thus saith the LORD, The labour of Egypt, and the 14
merchandise of Ethiopia, and the Sabeans, men of stature,
shall come over unto thee, and they shall be thine ; they

---

11. Ask...command ye me : man must not deem himself fit
to criticise the action of God as it is unfolded in history. Some
read the clause as an indignant question, making a slight change
in the Heb. : 'would ye question me...would ye command me?'

13. Certain Israelites have raised objection to the statement
that their redemption shall be effected through an alien monarch,
their hopes having been set on a Davidic king or Messiah. But
to criticise God is folly or worse; and the call to Cyrus is
reaffirmed.

in righteousness : see xlii. 6 note.

not...reward : Cyrus will act not from political or mercenary
motives, but prompted by an inward God-sent impulse: a view
which does not in any way clash with the belief (xliii. 3 f.) that
God will actually reward him.

14–17. In xliii. 3 f. the southern nations here mentioned are
regarded as the reward which Cyrus will receive for releasing
Israel. In the present passage, although it may be implied that
Cyrus conquers them, it is asserted that they and their tribute
('labour' and 'merchandise') are to be given to Israel. It is
wrong to demand complete harmony between such passages.
The prophet is concerned only to emphasise the thought of
Israel's coming glory, of which the crown will be the union of
humanity in the worship of Yahwe; the precise fashion of its
realisation is relatively unimportant.

shall go after thee ; in chains they shall come over : and
they shall fall down unto thee, they shall make supplication unto thee, *saying*, Surely God is in thee ; and there
15 is none else, there is no God.   Verily thou art a God that
16 hidest thyself, O God of Israel, the Saviour.   They shall
be ashamed, yea, confounded, all of them : they shall
17 go into confusion together that are makers of idols.   *But*
Israel shall be saved by the LORD with an everlasting
salvation : ye shall not be ashamed nor confounded world
without end.

18–25.   *The self-revelation of Yahwe is clear, and His*
purpose universal salvation.

18   For thus saith the LORD that created the heavens ;
he is God ; that formed the earth and made it ; he
established it, he created it not a waste, he formed it to
19 be inhabited : I am the LORD ; and there is none else.   I
have not spoken in secret, in a place of the land of
darkness ; I said not unto the seed of Jacob, Seek ye me

---

15.   Until the great deliverance, Yahwe has appeared to the
heathen as the weak god of an insignificant people.   His true
majesty and real character had been, as it were, hidden.

16.   At this point the prophet speaks, describing the situation
after Israel has been redeemed.   The verbs are better taken as
presents : 'they are ashamed...are put to confusion...Israel is
saved.

18–25.   The love of God extends throughout all the world
and is plain to those who are willing to look : such is the sublime
thought which inspires these verses.   The prophet has often
been obliged to regard the heathen in the hateful aspects of their
idolatry and their tyrannous oppression of Israel.   But the proud
nations now are humbled, and he turns to persuade them that
the tenderness of Yahwe reaches even unto them.

18. he created...inhabited : the Divine end in the act of
creation was the achievement of His purpose with man, not the
formation of a dead untenanted universe ('a waste,' cp. Gen. i. 2)

19.   To Israel God has spoken plainly, addressing His
appeal to the moral reason and not veiling Himself in unintelligible mysteries, as do the so-called gods of the heathen
peoples.

in vain : I the LORD speak righteousness, I declare things
that are right. Assemble yourselves and come ; draw 20
near together, ye that are escaped of the nations : they
have no knowledge that carry the wood of their graven
image, and pray unto a god that cannot save. Declare 21
ye, and bring *it* forth ; yea, let them take counsel together :
who hath shewed this from ancient time ? who hath
declared it of old ? have not I the LORD ? and there is no
God else beside me ; a just God and a saviour ; there
is none beside me. Look unto me, and be ye saved, 22
all the ends of the earth : for I am God, and there is none
else. By myself have I sworn, the word is gone forth 23
from my mouth *in* righteousness, and shall not return,
that unto me every knee shall bow, every tongue shall
swear. Only in the LORD, shall one say unto me, is 24
righteousness and strength : even to him shall men come,

---

in vain : without the possibility of success.

20, 21. As in xli. 1–4, 21–29, xliii. 9–13, the heathen are
confronted by the challenge of Yahwe's unique predictive power.
But here the prophet writes from the standpoint of the future :
the crisis is past, and the heathen are addressed as the survivors
of the storm, for whom nothing remains save to realise the plain
teaching of the victories of Cyrus and the exaltation of Israel.

20. that carry : in religious processions or on military cam-
paigns.

22–25. The idols are dumb, their champions for ever silenced.
Yahwe has gloriously proved His supreme and unique Godhead.
Now He moves on to the realisation of His ultimate aim, the
salvation of the entire human race.

23. shall not return : cp. lv. 11. His word is certain of
fulfilment, for God will not abandon His purpose.

24. Only...strength : render 'Only in Yahwe, shall one say,
have I righteousness and strength,' where 'righteousness' is
equivalent to 'salvation,' 'experience of deliverance.'

even...ashamed : better 'to Him shall come all who were
incensed against Him and shall be ashamed,' i.e. feel penitent
shame. The text, however, is not above suspicion, for the word
rendered 'be ashamed' is generally used as a threat, 'be put to
shame'; and in that case the thought seems unsuitable to the
context.

and all they that were incensed against him shall be
25 ashamed. In the LORD shall all the seed of Israel be
justified, and shall glory.

xlvi. *The fall of Babylon's gods and the steadfastness
of Yahwe.*

46   Bel boweth down, Nebo stoopeth ; their idols are upon
the beasts, and upon the cattle : the things that ye carried
2 about are made a load, a burden to the weary *beast.* They
stoop, they bow down together ; they could not deliver
the burden, but themselves are gone into captivity.

---

25. be justified : ' be righteous,' i.e. experience the blessings
of deliverance, as *v.* 24.

xlvi.   Our attention is now turned from the conqueror to the
conquered. As though witnessing the panic when the Babylonians
flee from their city, the prophet depicts the humiliation of the
idols which, so far from helping, are actually a hindrance to their
worshippers (*vv.* 1, 2), and draws the contrast between these
lifeless images and Yahwe, Israel's unfailing Helper (*vv.* 3–5).
Once more the impotence of the idols (*vv.* 6, 7), and the resistless
counsel of Yahwe (*vv.* 8–12) are emphasised.

1. Bel, Nebo : the chief deities of Babylon. ' Bel,' the
equivalent of Heb. 'Baal,' is a generic title 'Lord' appropriate
to any god, but in Babylon denoting specifically Marduk (or
'Merodach'), the tutelary deity of the city. Marduk was regarded
as king of the gods, arbiter of fate, and his seven-storied temple
in Babylon was known as the 'House of the Foundations of
Heaven and Earth.' Nebo, originally the arbiter of fate, was
given a place subordinate to Marduk, when Babylon secured the
headship of the Euphrates cities. It is possible that Nebo,
whose principal temple was at Borsippa near Babylon, was the
patron deity of the reigning Babylonian dynasty, as the word
formed part of the names of several monarchs of this period
(Nabo-polassar, Nebu-chadrezzar, Nabo-naïd).

the things…about : the images once carried in processions
through the city.

2. themselves…captivity : the prophet seems to allow a
distinction between the gods and their images. This may be an
unintentional adoption of the current heathen thought, or perhaps
he did regard the pretended gods as actual evil spirits. However
that may be, what matters is that they are powerless to oppose
Yahwe.

Hearken unto me, O house of Jacob, and all the 3
remnant of the house of Israel, which have been borne *by
me* from the belly, which have been carried from the
womb : and even to old age I am he, and even to hoar 4
hairs will I carry *you* : I have made, and I will bear ; yea,
I will carry, and will deliver.   To whom will ye liken me, 5
and make me equal, and compare me, that we may be
like ?   Such as lavish gold out of the bag, and weigh silver 6
in the balance, they hire a goldsmith, and he maketh it
a god ; they fall down, yea, they worship.   They bear him 7
upon the shoulder, they carry him, and set him in his
place, and he standeth ; from his place shall he not
remove : yea, one shall cry unto him, yet can he not
answer, nor save him out of his trouble.

Remember this, and shew yourselves men : bring it 8
again to mind, O ye transgressors.   Remember the former 9
things of old : for I am God, and there is none else ; *I
am* God, and there is none like me ; declaring the end 10
from the beginning, and from ancient times things that

---

3.   remnant...Israel : a reference to survivors of the Ten
Tribes, the Northern Captivity, is improbable.   Here, as else-
where in II Isaiah, 'Israel' seems to be used as a parallel to
Jacob, denoting the Jews of the Judaean kingdom.

have been borne : contrast *v. 2*.   The heathen deities are an
intolerable burden to their deluded worshippers ; but Israel is
sustained by Yahwe with unwearying fidelity.

5.   and make me equal : or 'so as to match me' : cp. xl. 18.

7.   one shall cry : better 'a man may cry,' but no help is
forthcoming in reply, cp. xlv. 20.

8.   shew yourselves men : marg. 'stand firm.'   The verb is
unknown and almost certainly the text is corrupt. . Read 'be
ye ashamed,' a slight alteration in the Heb.   .

ye transgressors : or 'ye rebels' : a term of strong indignation.
Notice the increasing anger of the prophet against certain of his
hearers—cp. xlv. 9 f. ; xlviii. 8 ; l. 11 ; and frequently in chs.
lv.–lxvi.

9.   the former...old : cp. xli. 22 ; xliv. 6–8.

for : better, as marg., 'that.'

are not *yet* done ; saying, My counsel shall stand, and
11 I will do all my pleasure : calling a ravenous bird from
the east, the man of my counsel from a far country ; yea,
I have spoken, I will also bring it to pass ; I have
12 purposed, I will also do it.   Hearken unto me, ye stout-
13 hearted, that are far from righteousness : I bring near my
righteousness, it shall not be far off, and my salvation
shall not tarry ; and I will place salvation in Zion for
Israel my glory.

      xlvii.   *Babylon is fallen!   A triumph song.*

      1–4.   *The depth of her coming shame.*

47   Come down, and sit in the dust, O virgin daughter

---

10. My counsel…pleasure : cp. xiv. 24 ; xliv. 28.
   11. a ravenous bird : i.e. Cyrus, the swiftness of whose
movements resembles the swoop of a bird of prey. The expression is peculiar, but cp. Jer. xlix. 22, Ez. xvii. 1 ff., where
Nebuchadrezzar is likened to an eagle.
   man of my counsel : not 'my counsellor,' for God needs
none, cp. xl. 13, 14 ; but the agent who carries out the Divine
plan.
   12. ye stouthearted : i.e. 'stubborn in unbelief' ;' but the
ordinary meaning of the word is 'resolute,' 'courageous,' which
does not suit the context. The text may be at fault, and the
LXX reads 'ye that have lost heart.'
   far from righteousness : if 'stubborn' be the right interpretation of the previous word, in the present phrase 'righteousness'
can only denote a right relationship to God, and the verse
reaffirms the rebuke of *v.* 8. It is probable, however, that the
word should bear the same meaning as in *v.* 13, where it stands
for the triumph secured by Yahwe's vindication of Israel's cause :
those who have lost heart imagine that salvation is far distant.
   13. Israel my glory : through Israel's prosperity, Yahwe
will manifest His glory. Another rendering is possible, 'I will
give my salvation to Zion, and my glory to Israel.'
   xlvii. 1–4. This chapter presents a song of exultant triumph
over Babylon whose downfall, though really future, is to the
prophet's mind so certain and so close at hand that he regards it
as already accomplished. The song consists of five strophes
(*vv.* 1–4, 5–7, 8–10[a], 10[b]–12, 13–15), each containing seven
lines, written in the elegiac metre regularly employed in laments

of Babylon; sit on the ground without a throne, O daughter of the Chaldeans : for thou shalt no more be called tender and delicate. Take the millstones, and 2 grind meal : remove thy veil, strip off the train, uncover the leg, pass through the rivers. Thy nakedness shall be 3 uncovered, yea, thy shame shall be seen : I will take vengeance, and will accept no man. Our redeemer, the 4 LORD of hosts is his name, the Holy One of Israel. Sit 5 thou silent, and get thee into darkness, O daughter of the

---

and in taunt-songs, such as the present : cp. the ode on the dead King of Babylon, in Is. xiv. 4-21. In the opening verses the proud city is commanded to take up its ignominious lot (*vv.* 1-4), on account of its past tyranny (*vv.* 5-7).

1-4. First strophe. Babylon is graphically personified. She has reigned as a queen, a delicate luxurious lady. She is now to be dragged from her throne, spoiled of her costly robes, and set to the degrading tasks of a slave-girl. The speaker is God.

1.   daughter of Babylon : i.e. Babylon, as 'daughter of Zion' is equivalent to Zion.

daughter of the Chaldeans : probably not 'Chaldea,' as the analogies of the preceding note would suggest, but rather 'Babylon.' The city was ruled by a Chaldean dynasty.

2.   Take the millstones : i.e. to grind corn : a task assigned to the meanest female slaves, cp. Ex. xi. 5. It was imposed on Samson as an extreme indignity, Jud. xvi. 21.

veil ‖ train : cp. iii. 18-23. Her royal garments are no garb for a slave's drudgery.

pass through the rivers : either, in the execution of her menial tasks, or else as one of the train of war-captives wading through the rivers on their path.

3.   Thy...seen : metrical reasons show clearly that this clause is an interpolation.

3, 4.   and will accept...redeemer : there is an error in the Heb. text : read 'and will not be entreated, saith our Redeemer....'

5-7. Second strophe. Babylon, chosen by God to be the agent of His chastisement of sinful Israel, has shown herself a reckless, pitiless tyrant. Her cruelty will recoil on her own head.

5.   silent ‖ darkness : the life and glitter of the Court is to be exchanged for solitude and gloom.

Chaldeans : for thou shalt no more be called The lady of
6 kingdoms. I was wroth with my people, I profaned mine
inheritance, and gave them into thine hand : thou didst
shew them no mercy ; upon the aged hast thou very
7 heavily laid thy yoke. And thou saidst, I shall be a lady
for ever: so that thou didst not lay these things to thy
heart, neither didst remember the latter end thereof.

8–12. *Nemesis! The certainty of ruin.*

8   Now therefore hear this, thou that art given to pleasures,
that dwellest carelessly, that sayest in thine heart, I am,
and there is none else beside me ; I shall not sit as a
9 widow, neither shall I know the loss of children : but
these two things shall come to thee in a moment in one
day, the loss of children, and widowhood : in their full
measure shall they come upon thee, despite of the
multitude of thy sorceries, and the great abundance
10 of thine enchantments. For thou hast trusted in thy

---

    lady of kingdoms: the flattery of her courtiers shall fall no
longer on her ears.
    6. I profaned : so long as Israel was 'holy to Yahwe,'
sanctified, she was inviolable (Jer. ii. 3); but Yahwe Himself
altered this relationship. He 'profaned,' unconsecrated, her ;
cp. Jer. xii. 7.
    7. remember the latter end thereof: i.e. reflect that her
cruelties might one day meet with retribution.
    8–12. In swift contrast the prophet recalls the arrogant
confidence which Babylon has displayed, but all her vaunted
wisdom and science will prove to be utterly futile. There is no
salvation possible for Babylon. (*vv.* 8–10ᵃ, Third strophe.
vv. 10ᵇ–12, Fourth strophe.)
    8. I am…me : Babylon describes herself in language appro-
priate only to the eternal God, cp. xlv. 6.
    a widow…children : i.e. a ruined city, abandoned by its gods
and inhabitants. Cp. xlix. 14 ff., li. 17, liv. 1, where the same
metaphors are applied to Zion.
    9. sorceries ‖ enchantments : Babylonia has justly been
described as the classic land of magic.
    10. trusted in thy wickedness : exercised her unscrupulous
tyranny without fear of retribution.

wickedness ; thou hast said, None seeth me ; thy wisdom
and thy knowledge, it hath perverted thee : and thou hast
said in thine heart, I am, and there is none else beside
me.   Therefore shall evil come upon thee ; thou shalt not 11
know the dawning thereof : and mischief shall fall upon
thee ; thou shalt not be able to put it away : and desolation shall come upon thee suddenly, which thou knowest
not.   Stand now with thine enchantments, and with the 12
multitude of thy sorceries, wherein thou hast laboured
from thy youth ; if so be thou shalt be able to profit, if so
be thou mayest prevail.

13–15.   *The futility of Babylon's devices.*

Thou art wearied in the multitude of thy counsels : let 13
now the astrologers, the stargazers, the monthly prognosticators, stand up, and save thee from the things that
shall come upon thee.   Behold, they shall be as stubble ; 14
the fire shall burn them ; they shall not deliver themselves

---

thy wisdom...knowledge : i.e. Babylon's magical arts (*vv.* 9,
12) and astrological lore (*v.* 13) perverted her judgment and
lulled her into a false security.

11.   the dawning thereof : read, as marg., 'how to charm
it away.'

12.   Let Babylon gather all her boasted resources for a last
desperate stand against Cyrus.

13–15.   Fifth strophe.   In the hour of trial all the toil which
Babylon has expended on her pseudo-sciences will avail her
nothing.   Certain destruction awaits her.

13.   let now...upon thee : rather 'let them now stand up
to save thee—the astrologers, the star-gazers, and those who
month by month foretell from what quarter (or simply 'what ')
things shall come upon thee.'

astrologers : lit. 'dividers of the heavens,' i.e. into the
Zodiacal signs and other constellations.

monthly prognosticators : compilers of monthly almanacs
indicating lucky and unlucky days, and predicting coming events.
The Babylonians had acquired profound knowledge of the movements of the heavenly bodies.

from the power of the flame : it shall not be a coal to
15 warm at, nor a fire to sit before. Thus shall the things
be unto thee wherein thou hast laboured : they that have
trafficked with thee from thy youth shall wander every
one to his quarter ; there shall be none to save thee.

xlviii. *A series of exhortations and rebukes addressed to Israel.*
1-11. *Hypocrisy and idolatry exposed and censured.*

48   Hear ye this, O house of Jacob, which are called by the

---

14. it shall not...before : better 'it shall be no coal whereat
to warm oneself, no fire to sit before,' an ironical way of saying
that the conflagration will be immense, the entire city will be
burnt up. But the expression is certainly strained, and, as it
also disturbs the rhythm, it may justly be suspected as an
interpolation.

15. they...with thee : or 'thy merchants.' It is true that
Babylon was world-famous for its vast commerce. The context,
however, calls rather for a reference to magic or astrology and the
rendering 'thy magicians,' which requires but a slight change in
Heb., is therefore plausible.

to his quarter : render 'straight before him.'

xlviii.   This chapter shows one remarkable peculiarity, esp.
in *vv.* 1-11. Closely interwoven with the familiar themes of
Yahwe's power in prediction, His creative majesty, the impending
fall of Babylon and the restoration of Israel, is a series of censures
addressed to Israel in a tone of bitter disappointment far sur-
passing that of the expressions used in xlii. 25, xliii. 24, xlv. 9.
In particular the explicit charge of idolatry (*v.* 5) seems to reflect
the feelings of a later period, and the general pessimism is hard
to reconcile with the expectation of immediate deliverance,
which is so characteristic of II Isaiah's work. Hence some
scholars consider that the phenomenon is best explained by
regarding these rebukes as a marginal or interlinear commentary supplied by a post-exilic writer, and afterwards by
error incorporated into the text itself. Ingenious though this
suggestion is, it remains difficult to see why the supposed com-
mentator has annotated only this chapter, leaving other very
similar passages untouched. The clauses suspected of being
interpolations are : 1^b, 2, 4, 5^b, 7^c, 8^b, 9, 10, 11 ('for how...
profaned '), 17-19.

1-11.   Israel is rebuked for its hypocrisy (*vv.* 1, 2) and the
idolatrous inclinations (*vv.* 4, 5, 8) which it has shown, despite
the clear tokens Yahwe has given of His power (*v.* 3), His
purpose (*vv.* 6, 7) and His faithfulness (*vv.* 9-11).

name of Israel, and are come forth out of the waters
of Judah ; which swear by the name of the LORD, and
make mention of the God of Israel, but not in truth, nor
in righteousness. For they call themselves of the holy 2
city, and stay themselves upon the God of Israel ; the
LORD of hosts is his name.   I have declared the former 3
things from of old ; yea, they went forth out of my mouth,
and I shewed them : suddenly I did them, and they came
to pass. Because I knew that thou art obstinate, and thy 4
neck is an iron sinew, and thy brow brass ; therefore 5
I have declared it to thee from of old ; before it came
to pass I shewed it thee : lest thou shouldest say, Mine
idol hath done them, and my graven image, and my
molten image, hath commanded them.   Thou hast heard 6
it ; behold all this ; and ye, will ye not declare it ?   I have
shewed thee new things from this time, even hidden

1, 2.   which are called...his name : possibly an interpolation.
If so, the opening words of *v.* 1, 'Hear ye this,' refer to the
declaration of *v.* 3.

1.   the waters : read, restoring a lost letter, 'the loins.'

truth...righteousness : contrast Zech. viii. 8.   The people
have the form but not the reality of worship.

2.   the holy city : again in lii. 1.   The standpoint is that of
a resident in Jerusalem, and this inference is supported by several
details in the language of the various verses considered interpolations.

3.   former things : the same argument as in xlii. 9, xliv. 8,
xlvi. 10.

4.   sinew : rather 'band.'

5.   therefore : render simply 'and.'

lest thou...commanded them : this direct charge is surprising,
if addressed to the exiles in Babylon.   However the book of
Ezekiel witnesses to the existence of idolatry amongst the Israelites
there, and in any case II Isaiah's repeated denunciations of the
folly of image worship suggest that there was real danger from
that source.   The clause accords with the tone of the verses
supposed to be interpolations, and its significance therefore
depends on the view we take of their origin and date.

6.   behold all this : the text is uncertain.

and ye, will ye : read 'and thou, wilt thou....'

new things : i.e. the announcements made in *vv.* 14, 15.

7 things, which thou hast not known. They are created
now, and not from of old; and before this day thou
heardest them not; lest thou shouldest say, Behold,
8 I knew them. Yea, thou heardest not; yea, thou knewest
not; yea, from of old thine ear was not opened: for
I knew that thou didst deal very treacherously, and wast
9 called a transgressor from the womb. For my name's
sake will I defer mine anger, and for my praise will
10 I refrain for thee, that I cut thee not off. Behold, I have
refined thee, but not as silver; I have chosen thee in the
11 furnace of affliction. For mine own sake, for mine own
sake, will I do it; for how should *my name* be profaned?
and my glory will I not give to another.

---

7. lest...I knew them: cp. the same expression in *v.* 5,
where it is said that God has foretold events long before their
occurrence, lest Israel should ascribe them to its idols. Here,
for the same reason, we are told that He predicts only on the
eve of the fulfilment. The two verses are not necessarily inconsistent: the prophet may wish to suggest that Israel would flee
from one excuse to the other, but that God debars it from
both. It is, however, much simpler to regard these clauses, 5ᵇ
and 7ᶜ, as interpolations.

8. heardest not: it is hard to say whether the prophet
means that Israel's insensibility arises from its own past obtuse-
ness, or from the fact that Yahwe only now reveals His purpose.

for I knew...womb: the note of pessimism seems out of
harmony with the feelings of chs. xl.–xlviii. It is much more
in keeping with various passages in chs. lv. ff.

9. For my name's sake: only the character of its God,
His mercy and faithfulness, has saved Israel from extinction,
cp. xliii. 25.

defer mine anger: the sentiment is obviously not appropriate
to the feelings of the Jews in the exilic period.

refrain: lit. 'muzzle,' *sc.* mine anger.

10. not as silver: either, by a process different from, more
severe than, that required for silver; or, 'not with silver,' i.e. with
silver as a result. Neither interpretation is satisfactory, and the
text is probably corrupt.

chosen thee: better, as marg., 'tried thee.'

11. for how...profaned: an exclamatory clause, and probably
a marginal gloss.

to another: *sc.* deity. If Israel's downfall were permanent,

12-16. Declaration of Yahwe's power and purpose.

Hearken unto me, O Jacob, and Israel my called : I am 12
he ; I am the first, I also am the last.   Yea, mine hand 13
hath laid the foundation of the earth, and my right hand
hath spread out the heavens : when I call unto them, they
stand up together.   Assemble yourselves, all ye, and hear ; 14
which among them hath declared these things?   The
LORD hath loved him : he shall perform his pleasure on
Babylon, and his arm *shall be on* the Chaldeans.   I, even 15
I, have spoken ; yea, I have called him : I have brought
him, and he shall make his way prosperous.   Come ye 16
near unto me, hear ye this ; from the beginning I have
not spoken in secret ; from the time that it was, there am
I : and now the Lord GOD hath sent me, and his spirit.

---

the glory of its God would apparently pass to the gods of its
conquerors.   This Yahwe will not permit.   Another view is
possible : Yahwe will make it clear that to Him and to Him
alone belongs the glory of Israel's restoration, cp. xlii. 8.

12-16.   In language closely resembling xliii. 9-12, xliv. 6-8,
Yahwe declares Himself to be the Creator of the universe and
promises the success of His chosen agent against Babylon.

13.   they stand up together : like servants waiting for their
Lord's command.

14.   Assemble yourselves : Israel, apparently, is still addressed.   Contrast xli. 1-4, xlv. 20, where the call for attention
is addressed to the Gentile nations.

The Lord...him : read, as marg., 'He whom Yahwe hath
loved shall....'

his arm (shall be on) the Chaldeans : the words in italics in the
text are not represented in the Heb.   An easy and suitable emendation yields the translation 'and on the seed of the Chaldeans.'

15.   and he...prosperous : better, with LXX, 'and I have
made his way prosperous.'

16.   from the beginning...am I : it is probable that the
pronoun 'it' refers to the subject under discussion, viz. Cyrus'
career ; in which case 'from the beginning' will denote, not the
beginning of the world, but the inception of the course of events
leading up to the coming deliverance.

and now...spirit : unquestionably an interpolation, as it breaks
the continuity of Yahwe's utterance.   For the sentiment, expressive
of the prophet's consciousness of his call, cp. lxi. 1 ; Zech. vii. 12.

and his spirit : i.e. equipped with His spirit.

17–19. A lament for the consequences of Israel's sinful past.

17 Thus saith the LORD, thy redeemer, the Holy One of
Israel : I am the LORD thy God, which teacheth thee to
profit, which leadeth thee by the way that thou shouldest
18 go. Oh that thou hadst hearkened to my commandments !
then had thy peace been as a river, and thy righteousness
19 as the waves of the sea : thy seed also had been as
the sand, and the offspring of thy bowels like the grains
thereof : his name should not be cut off nor destroyed
from before me.

20–22. The proclamation of freedom.

20   Go ye forth of Babylon, flee ye from the Chaldeans ;
with a voice of singing declare ye, tell this, utter it even
to the end of the earth : say ye, The LORD hath redeemed
21 his servant Jacob. And they thirsted not when he led
them through the deserts : he caused the waters to flow
out of the rock for them : he clave the rock also, and the

17–19. Beautiful as are the thoughts and imagery of this
pathetic passage, it is nevertheless highly probable that it is the
work of a later writer than II Isaiah. Verse 20 appears the true
sequel to *v.* 16ᵃ, and in general the yearning sadness of these
verses does not accord with the hope of immediate deliverance.

17. to profit: i.e. to thy profit, so as to prosper.

18. as a river: Israel's history resembles the intermittent
streams of Judaea, gleams of prosperity followed by long periods
of misfortune. Would that its success had been perennial, like
the current of a great river ! In lxvi. 12 the longing, here
regarded as a vanished hope, is spoken of as a blessing which
God is about to bestow.

20–22. Yahwe proclaims the word of release, and asserts His
providential care.

20. flee ye: not in fear, but in eagerness for freedom.

21. The verse continues the theme which the ransomed
people are to proclaim. The allusions are of course to the
wonders related of the Exodus from Egypt.

waters gushed out.   There is no peace, saith the LORD, 22
unto the wicked.

xlix.–lv.   *The Comforting of Zion.*
xlix. 1–6.   *A Song of the Servant* (II).

Listen, O isles, unto me ; and hearken, ye peoples, **49**
from far : the LORD hath called me from the womb ;
from the bowels of my mother hath he made mention
of my name : and he hath made my mouth like a sharp 2
sword, in the shadow of his hand hath he hid me ; and

---

22.   The verse is taken from lvii. 21, where it is suitable to
the context.   Its insertion here is due either to the author of the
other supposed interpolations in this chapter, or, more probably,
to a late editor who desired to indicate that a new section of the
book commences at ch. xlix.

xlix.–lv.   A new division of the prophecy.   The allusions to
Cyrus and Babylon, the assertions of Yahwe's unique Godhead,
the ridicule of the idols, all these familiar themes now disappear.
Moreover, although the writer's message is still one of joy and
comfort, the words of encouragement are specially addressed to
Zion-Jerusalem rather than to the Israelites themselves.   On the
other hand, chs. xlix.–lv. are united to xl.–xlviii. by the closest
similarity of style and vocabulary ; and the delineation of the
Servant of Yahwe constitutes an important link between the
two groups.   As to the bearing of these facts on the question of
authorship, date, and place of composition, see the Introd. p. xx f.

xlix. 1–6.   The second Song of the Servant.   In xlii. 1–4
God declared the election of His Servant and described the
manner of his working.   Here the Servant is himself the speaker,
first acknowledging his Divine vocation and equipment (*vv.* 1–3),
secondly—a new feature—relating an experience of struggle once
felt to have been in vain but now confidently endured with the
certainty of Yahwe's help (*v.* 4), and finally reciting, with full
comprehension of its magnificence, the task laid upon him by
Yahwe (*vv.* 5, 6).

1.   O isles: cp. note to xl. 15.   The Servant addresses the
distant nations, who are now all within the scope of his universal
mission.

2.   my mouth…sword : 'mouth,' the organ of speech : the
Servant is the ideal prophet.   Here he compares himself to a
favourite weapon kept in reserve for use at the critical moment
of the contest.   Gentle as his bearing may be (xlii. 2, 3) he has
also the power of sharp and effective speech.

he hath made me a polished shaft, in his quiver hath
3 he kept me close : and he said unto me, Thou art my
4 servant ; Israel, in whom I will be glorified. But I said,
I have laboured in vain, I have spent my strength for
nought and vanity : yet surely my judgement is with the
5 LORD, and my recompence with my God. And now
saith the LORD that formed me from the womb to be his
servant, to bring Jacob again to him, and that Israel
be gathered unto him : (for I am honourable in the eyes
6 of the LORD, and my God is become my strength :) yea,
he saith, It is too light a thing that thou shouldest be my

---

3. my servant ; Israel : the Suffering Servant is here expressly
termed Israel ; and those who seek to identify the Servant with
an individual are compelled to delete the word as a gloss. The
reasons adduced for so doing are unsatisfactory.

4. my judgement : better 'my right,' as in xl. 27.

5. And now : i.e. the hour has come when the revelation of
Yahwe's purpose, which His Servant is to achieve, shall be
disclosed in all its fulness.

to bring Jacob...unto him : here, and in *v.* 6, a distinction
is made between the Servant and Israel, since the restoration of
Israel is affirmed to be part of the Servant's task. This fact
presents a difficulty in the identification of the Servant with Israel.
The objection may be met in two ways. (1) Taking the text
as it stands, it may be said that if in the prophet's mind the
Servant stands for Israel in its ideal aspect, this aspect of the
nation has always had a certain concrete embodiment in the
persons of the faithful few. If so, the personification can be
thought of as actually a part of Israel, though ideally and
potentially the whole. As such, it is conceivable that the
Servant might be described as instrumental in the restoration
of Israel, the actual nation as a whole. (2) An alternative,
favoured by several scholars, is the view that in *v.* 5 the critical
clause ought properly to be translated 'in that He brought Jacob
back to Him and...,' thus making Yahwe and not the Servant
the subject. Others have argued with considerable force that
the clause 'to bring...unto him' is a gloss. See further the note
to *v.* 6.

be gathered : or 'be not swept away.'

for I am...strength : the clause should perhaps follow *v.* 3 :
translate 'and so I become honourable....'

6. It is too light...of Israel : lit. 'To raise up...and to restore
the preserved of Israel is too light a thing for thy being My

servant to raise up the tribes of Jacob, and to restore the
preserved of Israel : I will also give thee for a light to the
Gentiles, that thou mayest be my salvation unto the
end of the earth.

7–13. *Promises of Divine aid.*

Thus saith the LORD, the redeemer of Israel, *and* his 7
Holy One, to him whom man despiseth, to him whom

Servant (i.e. an insufficient task for so great an office). The
phrase 'for thy...Servant' is awkward metrically and may well
be an erroneous gloss. By its excision the perplexing distinction
which here, as in *v.* 5, seems to exist between the Servant and
Israel would disappear ; since, when the clause is thus emended,
it is Yahwe, and not the Servant, who declares the restoration
of Israel to be an inadequate manifestation of *His* power and
mercy ; and promises that—through the agency of Israel, His
Servant—He will also redeem the Gentile world.

Failing this expedient, the distinction between the Servant
and Israel can only be accounted for along the line indicated
in (1) of the note to *v.* 5 above.

I will...Gentiles: cp. xlii. 6.

that thou...salvation: so the LXX, but the marg. 'that my
salvation may be' is on the whole preferable. The verse is cited
by Paul and Barnabas in justification of their resolve to preach
Christ to the Gentiles (Acts xiii. 47).

7–13. A change in the metre occurs at this point, and at the
same time the outlook narrows from the universal to the national
standpoint. It is therefore probable that *v.* 6 is the conclusion
of the second Servant-song. At least it is clear that the task for
which the Servant in these verses is assured of the Divine succour
is simply the restoration of dispersed Israel. The sudden disap-
pearance of the universalist note, which in *vv.* 1–6 is the all-
important matter, is as evident as it is hard to explain. It is
tempting to suppose that *vv.* 7–12 are linking-verses supplied by
an editor, but on the other hand the style is precisely that of
II Isaiah and the connections which may be traced between
these so-called linking-verses and the four Songs seem too many
and too subtle to be suitably accounted for by the theory of
interpolation (cp. note to xlii. 5–9, and Introd. p. xx f.).

7. the redeemer...Holy One: so also in xli. 14, xliii. 14, etc.

to him...despiseth: 'to one despised of soul'; but possibly
the word 'soul' in this clause and 'nation' in the parallel
clause should be regarded as collective nouns. The phrase
will then be literally 'to the despised of men.'

the nation abhorreth, to a servant of rulers : Kings shall
see and arise ; princes, and they shall worship ; because
of the LORD that is faithful, *even* the Holy One of Israel,
8 who hath chosen thee.　Thus saith the LORD, In an
acceptable time have I answered thee, and in a day of
salvation have I helped thee : and I will preserve thee,
and give thee for a covenant of the people, to raise up
the land, to make them inherit the desolate heritages ;
9 saying to them that are bound, Go forth ; to them that
are in darkness, Shew yourselves.　They shall feed in the
10 ways, and on all bare heights shall be their pasture.　They
shall not hunger nor thirst ; neither shall the heat nor
sun smite them : for he that hath mercy on them shall
lead them, even by the springs of water shall he guide
11 them.　And I will make all my mountains a way, and
12 my high ways shall be exalted.　Lo, these shall come
from far : and, lo, these from the north and from the

---

to him...abhorreth : or 'to the abhorred of nations' (see
previous note).　It is significant that the sentiment of the verse
foreshadows the picture of the Suffering Servant in lii. 13–liii. 12.
arise ‖ worship : i.e. in token of respect, cp. lii. 15.
8.　acceptable time : rather 'time of favour,' cp. lxi. 2;
2 Cor. vi. 2.
a covenant of the people : the same phrase as in xlii. 6, where
see note.　The interpretation adopted there, viz. 'embodiment
or mediator of a covenant unto mankind,' finds support in the
LXX rendering of the present passage : 'a covenant of the
peoples.'
to raise up...heritages : is Yahwe or the Servant the subject
of these verbs?　Probably the former, cp. xlii. 7 (where the
same ambiguity of language occurs), and (for the thought)
xliv. 26.　Render therefore 'raising up...making them inherit....'
9.　feed in the ways : better, as LXX, 'in all ways,'
'everywhere.'
10.　the heat : reflected from the burning sands, or brought
by the fiery desert wind (Sirocco).　The rendering of the marg.
'mirage' is a mistake.
11.　my mountains...my high ways : i.e. the hills and roads
of Palestine.　The LXX reads 'all mountains...all high ways.'
**12.　The prophet anticipates an ingathering of the Dispersion
from all quarters, not simply from Babylon.　The point of

west ; and these from the land of Sinim.   Sing, O 13
heavens ; and be joyful, O earth ; and break forth into
singing, O mountains : for the LORD hath comforted his
people, and will have compassion upon his afflicted.

xlix. 14–l. 3. *The consolation of Zion.*

xlix. 14–21. *The restoration of her children.*

But Zion said, Jehovah hath forsaken me, and the Lord 14
hath forgotten me.   Can a woman forget her sucking 15
child, that she should not have compassion on the son
of her womb? yea, these may forget, yet will not I forget
thee.   Behold, I have graven thee upon the palms of 16
my hands ; thy walls are continually before me.   Thy 17
children make haste ; thy destroyers and they that made
thee waste shall go forth of thee.   Lift up thine eyes 18
round about, and behold : all these gather themselves
together, and come to thee.   As I live, saith the LORD,
thou shalt surely clothe thee with them all as with an

---

view is clearly that of a dweller in Jerusalem, but it is, of course,
possible that the prophet places himself there in fancy and in
reality is resident in Babylon.

land of Sinim : this name has given rise to much discussion.
It is now generally agreed that it does not refer to China, but
(with a slight modification of the Heb.) to ' Syene,' the modern
Assouan, situated in south Egypt.   There is evidence to show
that a Jewish colony existed there at this period.

13. A lyrical conclusion to the section *vv.* 1–12 ; somewhat
similar to xliv. 23.

14–21. In these beautiful verses Zion is addressed as the wife
of Yahwe and mother of its inhabitants.   Seemingly forsaken by
the Divine husband, she has mourned the loss of her children.
Now it is revealed to her that God has not cast her off for ever
and that her children will be restored.

15. Zion laments her children and deems herself forgotten of
God.   She is comforted by the assurance that even if her human
affection for her offspring were to cease, the Divine tenderness
would remain faithful to her.

17. **Thy children** : changing a vowel in the Heb., read, with
LXX, 'thy builders.'

19 ornament, and gird thyself with them, like a bride.   For,
as for thy waste and thy desolate places and thy land that
hath been destroyed, surely now shalt thou be too strait
for the inhabitants, and they that swallowed thee up shall
20 be far away.   The children of thy bereavement shall yet
say in thine ears, The place is too strait for me: give
21 place to me that I may dwell.   Then shalt thou say in
thine heart, Who hath begotten me these, seeing I have
been bereaved of my children, and am solitary, an exile,
and wandering to and fro? and who hath brought up
these? Behold, I was left alone; these, where were they?

22, 23.   *The Gentiles in humility restore the exiles of Zion.*

22   Thus saith the Lord GOD, Behold, I will lift up mine
hand to the nations, and set up my ensign to the peoples:
and they shall bring thy sons in their bosom, and thy

---

19.   For, as for...surely now: the difficulty of the construction in Heb. suggests that the concluding words of the first
clause ('thy...places and thy land') have dropped out of the
text; and that the words 'surely now' mark the beginning of
a new sentence.

too strait: i.e. too restricted in area for so large a population,
cp. Zech. ii. 4.

21.   Who hath begotten me these: better, as marg., 'borne.'
Jews born in exile ('children of Zion's bereavement,' *v.* 20) were
not regarded as sons of Zion until restored to her.   Then they
became hers by legal right, whilst the land in which they were
born might be described as having borne them for Zion (cp.
Gen. xvi. 1 f.).

solitary: better, as marg., ' barren.'

an exile...fro: the description is extremely inappropriate to
Zion.   The words are not found in the LXX, and may be
deleted as a gloss.

these...they: i.e. what foreign land was their dwelling place?
The Heb., however, is peculiar, and some prefer to make a
slight emendation, reading 'these, who then are they?'

22, 23.   The first of three short oracles confirming the promise
of consolation of Zion.

22.   they shall bring: the restoration is here depicted as an
act of spontaneous homage to Yahwe from the Gentiles. Cp. this
passage with xlv. 14 ff. and lx. 4, 8, lxvi. 20.

daughters shall be carried upon their shoulders. And 23
kings shall be thy nursing fathers, and their queens thy
nursing mothers : they shall bow down to thee with their
faces to the earth, and lick the dust of thy feet ; and thou
shalt know that I am the LORD, and they that wait for
me shall not be ashamed.

24-26.   The futility of opposing Yahwe's might.

Shall the prey be taken from the mighty, or the lawful 24
captives be delivered?　But thus saith the LORD, Even 25
the captives of the mighty shall be taken away, and
the prey of the terrible shall be delivered : for I will
contend with him that contendeth with thee, and I will
save thy children.　And I will feed them that oppress 26
thee with their own flesh ; and they shall be drunken

---

in their bosom : i.e. in the fold of the garment, where little
children were carried.

23.　nursing fathers : render 'guardians' or 'supporters.'

bow down ‖ lick the dust : expressions denoting an attitude of
complete submission, but not necessarily implying that Zion is
to play the *rôle* of a tyrant empire. Note, however, the difference
of feeling between the picture and the ideal presented by the
Servant-songs, in which the relationship of Israel to the Gentile
world is represented as that of purely spiritual service.

24-26.　A second oracle. Even if the hope of a voluntary
act of restoration by the Gentiles were not to be realised, Zion
need have no fear.　The mightiest nation is powerless to
withstand Yahwe.

24.　the lawful captives : lit. 'captives of the just one.'　No
satisfactory argument can be extracted from the text as it stands.
Accordingly it is desirable, by a slight change in Heb., to read
'the captives of the terrible one' (tyrant).　Two views of the
meaning are then possible :—(*a*) 'Can the captive of a mighty
man be set free?　Yes, for I, Yahwe, will overcome him.'
(*b*) 'Even the mightiest man may be conquered and his captive
set free ; but it is impossible for Me, Yahwe, to be defeated
and baulked of My purpose.'　The former interpretation is to be
preferred.

26.　feed them...own flesh : i.e. Zion's enemies shall perish
by mutual strife.

with their own blood, as with sweet wine: and all flesh
shall know that I the LORD am thy saviour, and thy
redeemer, the Mighty One of Jacob.

l. 1–3. *The broken covenant can be renewed.*

50   Thus saith the LORD, Where is the bill of your
mother's divorcement, wherewith I have put her away?
or which of my creditors is it to whom I have sold you?
Behold, for your iniquities were ye sold, and for your
2 transgressions was your mother put away. Wherefore,
when I came, was there no man? when I called, was
there none to answer? Is my hand shortened at all, that
it cannot redeem? or have I no power to deliver?

---

1. 1–3. A third oracle. No absolute bar exists to prevent
the renewal of God's covenant relationship with Israel. Why
then does there continue to be any doubt of His promise to
redeem?

1. Where is...away: according to the Jewish law (Deut. xxiv.
1–4) in the case of a separation between man and wife, the
separation was deemed absolute, if the husband gave the woman
a 'bill of divorcement.' But God has given no such document
to Zion, and He is therefore entitled to receive her again as wife.

which of my creditors: a father who sold his children in
liquidation of a debt thereby forfeited all parental authority over
them. Israel must not imagine that God was under any
external constraint when He delivered Israel into captivity. Of
His own free will He decreed the exile as a chastisement for
their sins, cp. lii. 3. Accordingly He is at liberty to renew the
parental relationship.

2. when I came...called: the past tenses suggest that the
opportunity for return has actually been given, and that the
exiles have failed to respond. If so, we have a clear indication
that the section is later than chs. xl.–xlviii., where the victory,
which is to open the path for return, is still in the future,
although to the eye of faith certain. But the 'coming and
calling' of Yahwe may refer simply to the prophet's prediction
of deliverance.

Is...shortened: the injustice of the doubt is exposed by the
following clauses which recall the manifestations of Yahwe's
might, as displayed by the portents of the Exodus or by the
phenomena of a stormy sky.

Behold, at my rebuke I dry up the sea, I make the
rivers a wilderness : their fish stinketh, because there
is no water, and dieth for thirst. I clothe the heavens 3
with blackness, and I make sackcloth their covering.

4–9. *A Song of the Servant* (III).

The Lord GOD hath given me the tongue of them that 4
are taught, that I should know how to sustain with words
him that is weary : he wakeneth morning by morning, he
wakeneth mine ear to hear as they that are taught. The 5
Lord GOD hath opened mine ear, and I was not rebellious,

4–9. The third Servant-song (cp. xlii. 1–4; xlix. 1–6;
lii. 13–liii. 12). From the style and sentiment of this passage it
is clear that the speaker is none other than the ideal Servant,
although the fact is not directly indicated. After affirming his
equipment for service and the daily inspirations granted him by
God (*v.* 4), he dwells on the fact that in the past he has had
to endure much suffering and contempt (*vv.* 5, 6), but has not
lost his faith that God will ultimately vindicate his cause (*vv.* 7–9).

4. tongue...taught: the ideal Servant will be of the prophetic
order (cp. xlix. 2), although the consolatory note of his message
is without precedent in the record of Israel's prophets.

sustain: the meaning of the verb is quite uncertain. The
marg., 'to speak a word in season,' follows the LXX.

he wakeneth...wakeneth: the doublet in the text is doubtless
a scribal error. Read simply ' in the morning (or 'morning by
morning') he wakeneth....'

5, 6. The first reference to the past sufferings of the Servant
has been given in xlix. 4. Here this feature is emphasised, and
we are thus prepared for the description of the innocent martyr
in ch. liii.

5. I was not rebellious: so emphatic an assertion of obedience
is clearly incompatible with the history of the actual historic
nation of Israel. The legitimate plea that only a relative, not an
absolute, perfection is affirmed, that relatively to other nations
Israel was innocent, seems inadequate, particularly if it be
desired to maintain that the Songs are by the same author as
v. 1 of this chapter and xlii. 18–25. The supposition that the
Servant is an individual would no doubt suit the present passage,
but is improbable for several reasons (see Introd. p. xxviii f.).
It is preferable to suppose that the idea in the writer's mind is
somewhat more complex. The explicit allusions to past sufferings

6 neither turned away backward. I gave my back to the
  smiters, and my cheeks to them that plucked off the hair :
7 I hid not my face from shame and spitting.   For the
  Lord GOD will help me ; therefore have I not been
  confounded : therefore have I set my face like a flint, and
8 I know that I shall not be ashamed.   He is near that
  justifieth me ; who will contend with me ? let us stand
  up together : who is mine adversary ? let him come near
9 to me.   Behold, the Lord GOD will help me ; who is
  he that shall condemn me ? behold, they all shall wax old
  as a garment ; the moth shall eat them up.

10, 11. *Exhortations appended to the Song.*

10   Who is among you that feareth the LORD, that obeyeth

(xlix. 2 ; l. 5, 6) and to an endowment for service already acquired
(l. 4) show that to some extent we have to do with historic
reality.   The situation may be met by the view that the Servant
represents an idealised Israel which "partly is, yet wholly is to
be."   The historic element arises through the consciousness in
the prophet's mind that his hope has had concrete form in the
sanctified minority by whom the nation's sufferings have been
accepted as part of God's will and interpreted in the light of
that faith.

  6. I gave : but, if so innocent, why this patient acquiescence
in suffering ? The question leads to the tremendous moral issue
which will be raised and answered in ch. liii. : how can a holy,
loving, and omnipotent God permit His faithful servant to endure
suffering even unto death ?

  my back...smiters : cp. Ps. cxxix. 3 ; Ezra ix. 3 ; Matt.
xxvi. 67, xxvii. 6, 7.

  7.   For...God : render 'But the Lord Yahwe.'

  8.   The metaphor of the verse is legal.   Israel's redemption,
or deliverance, is a verdict of acquittal, a declaration that the
defendant had right on his side, i.e. was 'just.'   Similarly,
according to the Hebrew notion, misfortune had to be construed
as a proof of guilt.   This forensic idiom is of importance for the
interpretation not only of many passages in the O.T., but also
for the thought of St Paul.

  9. condemn me : cp. Rom. viii. 33 f.

  10, 11. Judging from the tone of these two verses they are
an editorial addition, intended as an epilogue for the Servant-

the voice of his servant? he that walketh in darkness, and
hath no light, let him trust in the name of the LORD, and
stay upon his God.   Behold, all ye that kindle a fire, that 11
gird yourselves about with firebrands : walk ye in the
flame of your fire, and among the brands that ye have
kindled.   This shall ye have of mine hand ; ye shall lie
down in sorrow.

li. 1-16. *Encouragement for Israel.*

1-8. *Hope based on the faith of Abraham.*

Hearken to me, ye that follow after righteousness, **5**]

---

poem—*v.* 10 being a word of encouragement for the faithful,
v. 11 a threat to the impious.   Most probably both verses are
addressed to the Israelites, and it may be remarked that the
note of sharp division in the nation, between godly and ungodly,
suggests the post-exilic period and the conditions reflected in
parts of chs. lvi.–lxvi.

11. gird yourselves...firebrands : read perhaps 'set firebrands alight.'

in the flame : rather 'into the flame,' i.e. and thus perish in
your idolatrous rites.   Such is the usual interpretation, but there
is possibly an allusion to the strange but apparently authentic
fact that in certain forms of heathen-worship the devotees under
the stress of excitement become impervious to the ordinary
effects of heat on the human body.   If so, the prophet wishes
to assert that all the boasted marvels of their fire-walking will
fail to render the idolaters immune from the pains of the
retribution which God will certainly send upon them.

in sorrow : better 'in pain.'   Some render 'in the place of
torment.'   In any case the severity of tone is unlike 11 Isaiah,
and should be compared with lxvi. 24.

li. 1-8.   The strain of consolation is here resumed with an
exhortation to all faithful members of the nation.   They are
bidden to recollect how Abraham through faith became the
ancestor of Israel, and to expect that faith in Zion's restoration
will similarly be rewarded (*vv.* 1–3).   Let them believe that,
although the world were to perish, God's word would be
fulfilled (*vv.* 4–6) ; and let them cease to fear all human adversaries (*vv.* 7, 8).

1. righteousness : it is impossible to decide whether the
word here denotes 'success,' 'victory,' 'salvation' (as in *vv.* 5,
6, 8 ; cp. xlvi. 13) or is to be taken in an ethical sense, ' right

ye that seek the LORD : look unto the rock whence ye
were hewn, and to the hole of the pit whence ye were
2 digged. Look unto Abraham your father, and unto Sarah
that bare you : for when he was but one I called him, and
3 I blessed him, and made him many. For the LORD hath
comforted Zion : he hath comforted all her waste places,
and hath made her wilderness like Eden, and her desert
like the garden of the LORD ; joy and gladness shall
be found therein, thanksgiving, and the voice of melody.
4   Attend unto me, O my people ; and give ear unto
me, O my nation : for a law shall go forth from me, and
I will make my judgement to rest for a light of the
5 peoples.   My righteousness is near, my salvation is gone
forth, and mine arms shall judge the peoples ; the isles

---

conduct' (as in *v.* 7). The latter best suits the spirit of the
prophet's teaching.

rock...hewn...pit...digged: the patriarchs are the quarry, their
descendants the stones—a peculiar extension of the common
metaphor of terming a nation 'a house' (xlviii. 1).

2. Abraham...many : see Gen. xii. 2, xxii. 17.

3. Metrical reasons suggest that a line has dropped out of the
text immediately preceding this verse. The verbs are perfs. of
certainty ; render therefore 'shall surely comfort...shall make.'

wilderness ‖ desert : i.e. the barren districts of Judaea shall
become marvellously fertile. The comparison to the 'garden of
the Lord' occurs also in Gen. xiii. 10.

4, 5. The resemblance between these verses and xlii. 1–4 is
obvious, but there are also important differences. Here the
conversion of the heathen is represented as due to the direct
action of God, in xlii. 1–4 it is to be effected by the patient
persuasive influence of the Servant's example and teaching.
It may here be noted that in other passages (xlv. 6, 14–17) the
world-conversion is ascribed to the immediate effect of Cyrus'
victories, whilst in the later chapters of the book it results from
the impression made on the heathen by the glory of the restored
Jerusalem (lx. 2, 3).

4. a law : rather 'instruction.'

4, 5. my judgement...near : for 'judgement' render 'ordinance' or 'religion.' A better reading is that in the LXX,
'and my judgement for a light of the peoples. In an instant
my righteousness,' etc.

shall wait for me, and on mine arm shall they trust. Lift up your eyes to the heavens, and look upon the 6 earth beneath : for the heavens shall vanish away like smoke, and the earth shall wax old like a garment, and they that dwell therein shall die in like manner : but my salvation shall be for ever, and my righteousness shall not be abolished.

Hearken unto me, ye that know righteousness, the 7 people in whose heart is my law ; fear ye not the reproach of men, neither be ye dismayed at their revilings. For 8 the moth shall eat them up like a garment, and the worm shall eat them like wool : but my righteousness shall be for ever, and my salvation unto all generations.

9-16. Hope based on Yahwe's ancient deeds of power.

Awake, awake, put on strength, O arm of the LORD ; 9

---

5. on mine arm...trust: i.e. they hope for My active intervention ('arm'). On metrical grounds the clause is suspected to be a gloss.

The verse is a wonderful expression of faith. Though the apparently indestructible mass of the earth and the overarching heaven were to be dissolved, the prophet believes that Yahwe somehow would effect His purpose of love to man : the things that are seen are to him temporal, but the things that are unseen are eternal.

6. vanish away: lit. ' be torn to rags.' Translate ' shall be dissolved.'

in like manner: rather, as marg., ' like gnats,' but the meaning of the Heb. is uncertain.

7. reproach: i.e. scorn, reviling.

9-16. Again let the timorous followers of Yahwe recall the traditions of His might exerted in primaeval times (*v.* 9) and at the Exodus (*v.* 10). Only one inference can be drawn—Israel will be restored to Zion by Yahwe (*v.* 11), and will be comforted and delivered from all fear of her adversaries (*vv.* 12-16).

9. An appeal to God to exercise His power. The speaker may be either the prophet himself, or the Israelites whose faith, we may suppose, has now been quickened by the declarations of the preceding verses.

arm of the Lord: the symbol of His power, cp. *v.* 5.

awake, as in the days of old, the generations of ancient
times.   Art thou not it that cut Rahab in pieces, that
10 pierced the dragon?   Art thou not it which dried up the
sea, the waters of the great deep; that made the depths
11 of the sea a way for the redeemed to pass over? And
the ransomed of the LORD shall return, and come with
singing unto Zion; and everlasting joy shall be upon
their heads: they shall obtain gladness and joy, *and*
sorrow and sighing shall flee away.

12 I, even I, am he that comforteth you: who art thou,
that thou art afraid of man that shall die, and of the son
13 of man which shall be made as grass; and hast forgotten
the LORD thy Maker, that stretched forth the heavens,

---

cut Rahab in pieces...dragon: (1) Rahab, a dragon-monster,
represents or personifies the primaeval Chaos of waters; and the
'dragon,' mentioned in the parallel clause, is either a synonym
for Rahab or is one of Rahab's helpers (Job ix. 13).   The terms
belong to the realm of early Semitic mythology, according to
which the universe as we know it (dry-land, sea, and sky) was
created by the victory of a Divine Being, who overcame this
Chaos (Rahab) by dividing ('cut in pieces,' 'pierced') its waters.
It may well be that the prophet has this story in mind, and
claims for Yahwe the glory of the conquest of Chaos; but
(2) another interpretation of the passage is possible. When
Egypt became to the Israelites the incarnation of evil, the terms
'Rahab' and 'The Dragon' were applied to that empire, and
some consider that the words are used here only with this historical
significance.   The present writer thinks that the Creation story
is alluded to in *vv.* 9, 10ᵃ, and that the thought of how the
primaeval waters were divided by Yahwe afforded an easy
transition to (*v.* 10ᵇ) the story of the crossing of the Red Sea.

11.   This verse is found also at xxxv. 10, where clearly the
sentiment is in its proper setting.   Here it must be regarded
as a gloss added by a reader or scribe as a comment on the
word 'redeemed.'

12-16.   The conclusion, drawn above from the faith of
Abraham, follows likewise from the recollection of God's
creative might.   Beyond all doubt, He will protect and restore
His people.

12.   made as grass: lit. 'given up as grass,' allowed to be
destroyed.

13.   forgotten...earth: not that Israel has forgotten to

and laid the foundations of the earth ; and **fearest**
continually all the day because of the fury of the oppressor,
when he maketh ready to destroy? and where is the fury
of the oppressor? The captive exile shall speedily be 14
loosed ; and he shall not die *and go down* into the pit,
neither shall his bread fail. For I am the LORD thy God, 15
which stirreth up the sea, that the waves thereof roar :
the LORD of hosts is his name. And I have put my 16
words in thy mouth, and have covered thee in the shadow
of mine hand, that I may plant the heavens, and lay the
foundations of the earth, and say unto Zion, Thou art my
people.

li. 17–lii. 12.   *Encouragement for desolate Zion.*

li. 17–23.   *The end of her tribulation.*

Awake, awake, stand up, O Jerusalem, which hast 17

worship Him, but that it has failed to remember and to rely
on His marvellous power, cp. xl. 22, etc.

fearest...oppressor: the clause is generally regarded as an
indication that these verses were written before the fall of the
Babylonian empire. But the expression 'oppressor' is too vague
to justify so definite a conclusion. Although our knowledge of
the period after the accession of Cyrus in 538 B.C. is confused
and very incomplete, there were certainly many years when the
Jews of Jerusalem longed for a general return of the Dispersion
and stood in fear of Gentile oppression.

and where...oppressor: a weak ending to the verse, but it is
quite likely that the text here as in the foll. clause is unsound.

14. The captive exile: lit. 'the crouching one,' i.e. the
Israel of the Dispersion. There is no reason to limit the
reference to the exiles in Babylon. The evidence of the LXX
suggests that the original reading has been lost.

16. plant the heavens: in view of *v.* 6, the creation of
a new heaven, which is implied by the text, cannot be called
a quite improbable idea for the prophet to entertain ; but the
metaphor 'plant' is very strange. It is preferable, with a slight
change in Heb., to read the customary phrase 'stretch out'
(cp. *v.* 13 ; xl. 22, etc.), and to regard the verbs of the verse as
gerundial infs., translating : 'stretching out...laying...saying' ;
the reference then being, as above, to the primaeval creation.

drunk at the hand of the LORD the cup of his fury ; thou
hast drunken the bowl of the cup of staggering, and
18 drained it.   There is none to guide her among all the
sons whom she hath brought forth ; neither is there any
that taketh her by the hand of all the sons that she hath
19 brought up.   These two things are befallen thee ; who
shall bemoan thee ? desolation and destruction, and the
20 famine and the sword ; how shall I comfort thee ?   Thy
sons have fainted, they lie at the top of all the streets, as
an antelope in a net ; they are full of the fury of the LORD,
21 the rebuke of thy God.   Therefore hear now this, thou
22 afflicted, and drunken, but not with wine : thus saith thy
Lord the LORD, and thy God that pleadeth the cause
of his people, Behold, I have taken out of thine hand the
cup of staggering, even the bowl of the cup of my fury ;
23 thou shalt no more drink it again : and I will put it

---

ll. 17–lii. 12.   In this section the prophet addresses his consolatory message to the ruined city itself.   The passage, which
is written in the elegiac metre, falls into two divisions, (a) *vv.* 17–
23, (b) lii. 1, 2, 7–12.

17–23.   Zion is pictured as a woman lying insensible, overcome
by the bitter draught from the cup of God's anger.   She is
commanded to rise and learn that the fate which has reduced
her to such abject misery will be the portion of her enemies.

17. drunk...fury : the metaphor first occurs in Jer. xxv.
15 ff., where Jeremiah is bidden by God to take the cup
of the Divine fury and make the nations drink from it.
Cp. Rev. xiv. 10.

bowl of the cup : read simply 'bowl' : so also in *v.* 22.

18.   A change of metre and the fact that Jerusalem is referred
to in the 3rd person (contrast *vv.* 17 and 19) strongly suggest
that the verse is not part of the original text.

19. These two things : one, the ruin of her buildings
('desolation and destruction'), the other, the death of her
citizens (by 'famine and sword ').

shall I comfort : read, with the ancient versions, 'Who
shall comfort thee ? '

23. Bow down...go over : a graphic simile for utter humiliation.   The allusion is to the custom of Eastern conquerors who
walked or rode over the backs of captive foes.

into the hand of them that afflict thee ; which have said
to thy soul, Bow down, that we may go over : and thou
hast laid thy back as the ground, and as the street, to
them that go over.

lii. 1-12.   *The triumph of Zion.*

Awake, awake, put on thy strength, O Zion; put on **52**
thy beautiful garments, O Jerusalem, the holy city: for
henceforth there shall no more come into thee the uncircumcised and the unclean.   Shake thyself from the 2
dust; arise, sit thee down, O Jerusalem: loose thyself
from the bands of thy neck, O captive daughter of Zion.

For thus saith the LORD, Ye were sold for nought; and 3
ye shall be redeemed without money.   For thus saith the 4

---

lii. 1-12. In this, the second, section of the exhortation to
Zion, the restored city is commanded to don a festal robe,
befitting her joyous state (*vv.* 1, 2). In *vv.* 7-12 the prophet
pictures the reception at Jerusalem of the glorious tidings of
deliverance.   The passage pulsates with the passion of the
prophet's faith and joy. On *vv.* 3-6 see note below.

1. uncircumcised...unclean. Not that all Gentiles are to
be excluded from the city, but simply that Zion will never again
suffer the violent entry of a foreign conqueror. Set free from
the pollution of an alien governor or garrison, she must array
herself in robes appropriate to her new sanctity.

2. sit: i.e. on thy throne.   But some favour a reading,
'Arise, O captive Jerusalem,' which involves but a small change
in Heb.

3-6. The Heb. here changes from poetry to prose, metrical
structure being resumed at *v.* 7. At the same time the subject
passes from Zion to the sufferings of the people of Israel, which
God will no longer tolerate.   The verses are reasonably
regarded as an interpolation, added perhaps to supply a gap in
the MSS.

3. For: the connection with the preceding verses is found in
the idea that the redemption just alluded to is the redress for
past wrongs.

redeemed without money: when God delivered Israel to
the Babylonians, the transaction was not in the nature of a
forced sale, no debt was thereby liquidated, He had received no
equivalent (see notes l. 1).   Consequently He is free to resume
possession without payment.

E.

5

Lord GOD, My people went down at the first into Egypt
to sojourn there: and the Assyrian oppressed them with-
5 out cause.   Now therefore, what do I here, saith the
LORD, seeing that my people is taken away for nought?
they that rule over them do howl, saith the LORD, and
6 my name continually all the day is blasphemed.   Therefore my people shall know my name: therefore *they shall*
know in that day that I am he that doth speak; behold,
it is I.

7   How beautiful upon the mountains are the feet of him
that bringeth good tidings, that publisheth peace, that
bringeth good tidings of good, that publisheth salvation;
8 that saith unto Zion, Thy God reigneth!   The voice of
thy watchmen! they lift up the voice, together do they
sing; for they shall see, eye to eye, when the LORD

---

4.   without cause: the statement is strange, and conflicts
with the usual view that Israel suffered for its sins (xl. 2; xlii. 24;
xliii. 27 f.; li.).   Possibly the Heb. may be rendered 'for
nothing.'   The LXX reads 'with violence.'

5.   what...here: lit. 'What is there to me here?'   What
place are we to understand by 'here'?   Possibly Jerusalem:
God feels that His presence there is useless, since His people
are elsewhere, but it is an objection that in several places Yahwe
is represented as having forsaken Zion.   Or 'here' might mean
the 'land of exile,' or 'the present situation,' or even 'heaven'
as the abode of God.   The point cannot be determined with
certainty, and is of consequence only if the verses are not a late
interpolation.

6.   Delete the second 'therefore' and the words in italics.

7–12.   The metre and theme of *vv.* 1, 2 are now resumed.
The prophet anticipates the scene when Zion receives the good
news of Yahwe's triumphal act.

7.   The herald is seen hastening over the hills with his
message of victory.   How welcome his advent!   Cp. xl. 9;
xli. 27; and Rom. x. 15.

Thy God reigneth: at last there is once more a King in
Zion, and the King is—God Himself!

8.   The voice...watchmen: render 'Hark! Thy watchmen,'
cp. xl. 3, 6.

eye to eye: i.e. clearly.   A strong phrase but not to be

returneth to Zion. Break forth into joy, sing together, 9
ye waste places of Jerusalem : for the LORD hath comforted his people, he hath redeemed Jerusalem. The 10
LORD hath made bare his holy arm in the eyes of all the
nations ; and all the ends of the earth shall see the
salvation of our God. Depart ye, depart ye, go ye out 11
from thence, touch no unclean thing ; go ye out of the
midst of her ; be ye clean, ye that bear the vessels of
the LORD. For ye shall not go out in haste, neither 12
shall ye go by flight : for the LORD will go before you ;
and the God of Israel will be your rearward.

---

pressed to mean that God Himself will be visible. The
watchers will perceive the glory of the scene as a whole, and
perhaps the prophet thinks that there will be visible some
wonderful phenomenon indicative of the presence of God.

9. hath comforted ‖ hath redeemed : perfs. of certainty,
cp. li. 3.

10. hath made bare : in readiness for the conflict which
is to precede the triumphal entry. Remark the boldness of the
metaphor, cp. xl. 10 ; li. 9.

11. thence : the command is obviously addressed to exiled
Israelites, but whether 'thence' refers simply to Babylon or
more generally to any Gentile land where Jews resided is an
open question : cp. the word 'here' (v. 5). The allusion to the
'vessels of the Lord' (see note below) greatly strengthens the
presumption that Babylon is referred to. If so, it follows that,
since the exodus of the Jews from it is still a future event, no
appreciable difference of time or standpoint can separate this
prophecy from the group xl.–xlviii.

be ye clean : ceremonial purity is naturally required of those
who carry Yahwe's sacred vessels to the purified city, but all
who take part in the procession which Yahwe leads are 'holy'
and must 'touch no unclean thing.'

vessels : if 'thence' in v. 10ª be Babylon, the reference here
would be specifically to the sacred vessels of Solomon's Temple,
which were carried off by Nebuchadrezzar, and it would follow
that the passage could not be of later date than the edict of
Cyrus, 537 B.C.—provided the statement in Ezra i. 1–7 be
historically correct.

12. not...in haste : contrast the account of the flight from
Egypt (Exod. xii. 33, 39).

5—2

lii. 13–liii. 12.   *A Song of the Servant* (IV).

lii. 13–15.   *Yahwe promises the vindication of His Servant.*

13   Behold, my servant shall deal wisely, he shall be exalted
14   and lifted up, and shall be very high.   Like as many

---

lii. 13–liii. 12.   The fourth Servant-song.   In the first of
these passages (xlii. 1–4) God called attention to His ideal
Servant, announced his universal mission, and described his
gentle, but none the less undaunted, manner of working.   In
the second (xlix. 1–6) the Servant himself declared his conscious
acceptance of the task, and his faith—despite past tribulations—
that he would yet achieve his glorious end.   In the third (l. 4–9)
the Servant was again the speaker.   After asserting his Divine
equipment for the task, and recalling the persecution he has
endured in Yahwe's cause, he reaffirmed his certainty that in the
end Yahwe would vindicate his faith.   This fourth Song might
be entitled the Servant's transfiguration, for a dazzling and
unforeseen light is now shed upon the career of the strange and
fascinating figure.   Again the voice of God is heard (lii. 13–15),
proclaiming to the astonished world that the victim upon whom
cruelty and contempt have been heaped, is in very truth the
chosen, honoured, and innocent Servant of the Most High, and
is about to be raised to the highest glory.   Then, in the wonder
of this transformation, an unimagined depth of meaning in his past
suffering will be revealed.   It will be seen that not the Servant
but his persecutors were guilty, that his suffering was theirs by
right.   Nevertheless in the spirit of love he has endured the
persecution even unto death, to the end that they may be saved.
This blameless sacrifice has not been made in vain, for God
will quicken His Servant from death and gladden him with the
realisation of his hopes.   Whatever the prophet may have
sought to represent by this marvellous Personification (see
Introd. pp. xxvii ff.), it is evident that his inspired words portray
a character so perfect in holiness and self-sacrifice as to be a
most wonderful anticipation of the life, the suffering, and the
risen glory of the Lord Jesus Christ.

The passage is best divided into three sections : lii. 13–15;
liii. 1–9 ; liii. 11, 12.   The metre is the same as that found in
the first two Songs, but the original number of quatrains is
uncertain.   Here and there a word seems to have dropped out
of the text, and unfortunately in the last part of ch. liii. the
state of the text is such that only the general sense of the
passage can be relied upon.

13–15.   The speaker is Yahwe.   From terrible disfigure-
ment, His Servant shall be made so glorious that the nations
and their kings will be filled with amazement.

were astonied at thee, (his visage was so marred more
than any man, and his form more than the sons of men,)

---

13. Behold: to whom does Yahwe speak? The question is of
great importance in considering the problem of the Servant's
identity. Those who in the past have ill-treated and misunder-
stood the Suffering Servant, but to whom now the revelation of
his true glory is declared, and who in ch. liii. give utterance to
their sorrow, their penitence, and their measureless debt to
him—are they the heathen nations or the unbelieving in Israel?
If the latter, the sharp division which ch. liii. then reveals between
the faithless, though now repentant, element in Israel and the
Servant is clearly so important that the Servant could only be
regarded as a fraction or an aspect of the nation—either the
godly section of the people, or a purely ideal Israel distinct from
the actual nation.

It seems to the present writer not only tenable but even
more natural to regard the heathen as the persons addressed in
vv. 13–15 and as the speakers in ch. liii.; in which case there is
no need to depart from the theory hitherto maintained regarding
the Servant's identity: that he is historic Israel, partly real
partly ideal, as it appears from the standpoint of the prophet's
faith, experiences, and hopes. That the announcement of
vv. 13–15 is made to the heathen world in general is the
natural inference from the whole tone of those two verses, and
in particular from *v.* 15 with its references to the 'many nations'
and to 'kings.' And it is reasonable to suppose that liii. 1 ff.
sets forth the astonishment of the monarchs and peoples to whom
the startling revelation alluded to in lii. 15 has just been made.
In the other Servant-songs the unique feature is precisely the
universality of the Servant's mission. It would be strange, if in
the fourth Song this central matter were barely hinted at and the
climax were made to be his acknowledgement by the godless in
Israel. Whereas it seems entirely suitable that the good tidings
of his exaltation should be told to the redeemed world and its
kings, and that the conclusion should be an expression of their
penitence and their joy. It is urged in objection that such
wonderful penitence and spiritual appreciation as is found in
ch. liii. is incredible on heathen lips, but surely this overlooks
the vital point that the speakers are *converted* heathen, who have
been startled out of their spiritual sleep, and whose eyes are now
open to perceive the full truth.

shall deal wisely: or, as marg., 'shall prosper,' an unusual
meaning for the verb, but somewhat more suitable in this
context. The accumulation of verbs in the verse is curious,
and has led to the ingenious suggestion (involving but a small
alteration in Heb.) that we should read 'Israel' in place of

15 so shall he sprinkle many nations ; kings shall shut their mouths at him : for that which had not been told them shall they see ; and that which they had not heard shall they understand.

liii. *The recognition of the Servant's glory.*

1–8. *His suffering described and explained.*

53 Who hath believed our report ? and to whom hath the

'shall deal wisely.' This reading, taken in conjunction with xlix. 3, would put it beyond doubt that the Servant personified the nation in some sense, but the conjecture is unfortunately not supported in the ancient versions.

14. thee : the LXX has the 2nd pers. throughout the verse, but the present solitary occurrence of the 2nd for the 3rd pers. in the Heb. must be regarded as a slip : read therefore 'him.'

his visage...men : the parenthetical construction is very awkward. It is therefore possible that the words have been misplaced, and originally followed liii. 2, where they would suit well. Translate 'so (or 'because') marred from that of man was his aspect, and his form from that of the sons of men.'

15. so...sprinkle : the apodosis to the clause 'like as...,' *v.* 14. In place of 'sprinkle'—a meaning which cannot legitimately be placed on the verb—read perhaps 'shall startle' (lit. 'cause to leap').

kings...mouths : in token of respect and wonder, cp. Job xxix. 9 f.

for that...understand : i.e. all had been misled by the apparent humiliation of the Servant, so that they had not in any way anticipated his unprecedented glory. For 'understand,' translate 'perceive.' Cp. the N.T. quotation, Rom. xv. 21.

liii. The chapter is in form a confession on the part of those who have so grievously misconceived the Servant and who now recognise that they have been redeemed through his voluntary suffering. The speakers are the heathen nations and their kings (see note on lii. 13), giving utterance to the astonishment of which lii. 13–15 speaks.

The recollection of the Servant's afflictions (*vv.* 1–4) and their own blindness to its true meaning (*vv.* 5, 6) is set in contrast to his utter devotion (*vv.* 7–9) ; and finally the inner glory of the Servant's achievement is revealed in a declaration of its effects and its reward (*vv.* 10–12).

1. Who...report : the ambiguous phrase 'our report' is to be interpreted as in the marginal trans. 'that which we have heard,' i.e. the startling announcement, otherwise incredible,

arm of the LORD been revealed? For he grew up before 2
him as a tender plant, and as a root out of a dry ground:
he hath no form nor comeliness; and when we see him,
there is no beauty that we should desire him. He 3
was despised, and rejected of men; a man of sorrows,
and acquainted with grief: and as one from whom
men hide their face he was despised, and we esteemed
him not.

---

but now made indubitable by Yahwe's express declaration, that
the despised Servant is about to be crowned with glory. The
simple perf. 'hath believed' is not quite suitable to the view
that the speakers in liii. are the heathen addressed in lii. 13–15,
for obviously the intention is not to assert that even now they
have disbelieved Yahwe's words. This difficulty is removed by
translating 'Who could have believed,' a legitimate though rare
use of the Heb. tense.

to whom ..revealed: i.e. who could have (or 'did') anticipate
Yahwe's intention of actively manifesting His power? Cp. li. 9.

2. For: lit. 'and,' marking the commencement of a narrative.

before him: i.e. before Yahwe, as though Israel, like a weakly
plant struggling in uncongenial soil, has been ignored by all
except Yahwe. It is preferable, however, to make a slight
alteration and read 'before us.'

dry ground: possibly the metaphor is intended to represent
the deadening influences of Israel's life in its exilic homes.

he hath...desire him: better 'he had no form nor majesty
that we should look upon him, no aspect such that we should
desire him.' See also the note 'his visage...men,' lii. 14.

3. So terrible were the Servant's afflictions, that men were
actually repelled by his appearance, turning away as they would
from a leper.

rejected of men: or, as marg., 'forsaken.' The phrase
may be taken either *actively* 'man-forsaking' or *passively*
'man-forsaken.' In either case the point is that of enforced
isolation from the gladness of human society.

sorrows ‖ grief: here and in *v.* 4, render 'pains,' 'sickness,'
the literal signification of the words. It seems right to maintain
the simile of the verse, although of course the notion of disease
is ultimately metaphorical.

as one...face: following LXX, the marg. reads 'he hid as it
were his face from us.' This is grammatically possible, but in
meaning is less suitable to the tone of the passage.

4   Surely he hath borne our griefs, and carried our sorrows:
    yet we did esteem him stricken, smitten of God, and
5   afflicted.   But he was wounded for our transgressions, he
    was bruised for our iniquities : the chastisement of our
    peace was upon him ; and with his stripes we are healed.

4-6. These verses, in which the true significance of the Servant's
career is disclosed, preserve what may be considered to be the
most sublime expression of religious faith which has come down
to us from the pre-Christian world.   About this period it had
become clear to certain minds that misfortune was not necessarily,
as the ancient creed had supposed, a token of guilt, and the
problem of *innocent* suffering was felt to be the greatest barrier
against belief in a holy and loving God.   In the book of Job
the question is worked out from the standpoint of an individual,
and there the answer is made that the consideration of how
infinitely the power and glory of God surpasses our imagination
ought to make us trustful that with Him there is some wise and
perfect solution of our mystery, although the problem in itself
remains insoluble to the human intelligence.   Here the same
question is treated from the national point of view, and a
solution is actually discovered—in the sublime conception of
vicarious suffering.   The burdens entailed by the sins of the
heathen world fall upon the Servant with crushing severity just
in so far as he is ideally serving a God, who wills that no man
should perish.   He shares the Divine toil and agony for the
sinful world.   But the suffering will not be endured in vain, nor
will the surrender of life itself pass unrewarded ; for in the end
God will glorify His Servant, and the heathen nations, perceiving
the amazing love revealed by such suffering, innocently and un-
grudgingly borne for their sakes, will realise the true nature of
him whom they despised.   In penitence they will acknowledge
his merit and their own guilt.   Thus by the path of suffering
the Servant's task will be crowned with success, and the way of
Yahwe, so mysterious whilst only the outward aspect of the case
was perceived, will be seen to have its justification when the
ultimate vindication of the Servant and the redemptive efficacy
of his sacrifice are manifested to all the world.

4. stricken: the word is characteristically employed with
reference to the affliction of a deadly disease, especially
leprosy.

5. wounded, bruised: better 'pierced,' 'crushed.'

  chastisement...peace : the pain through which our well-being
has been effected.

All we like sheep have gone astray; we have turned 6
every one to his own way; and the LORD hath laid on
him the iniquity of us all.

7–9. *The martyrdom of the Servant.*

He was oppressed, yet he humbled himself and opened 7
not his mouth; as a lamb that is led to the slaughter,
and as a sheep that before her shearers is dumb; yea, he
opened not his mouth. By oppression and judgement he 8
was taken away; and as for his generation, who *among
them* considered that he was cut off out of the land of the

---

6. like sheep: cp. Matt. ix. 36; Luke xv. 4.

hath laid...iniquity: better, as marg., 'hath made to light
on him the guilt.'

7–9. A wonderful description of the Servant's patient
endurance in the execution of his task.

7. oppressed: i.e. through the cruelties practised against him
by human enemies. There is no real contradiction between this
and the statement of *v.* 4 that he was esteemed to be 'smitten
of God,' which phrase simply means that his calamities were
regarded as ultimately due to the indifference or hostility of
God, quite apart from the minor question whether the Divine
stroke reached him through human agency or not.

yea...mouth: metrical considerations make it probable that
the words are accidentally repeated from the first part of the
verse.

8. Unfortunately the Heb. text here and in the rest of the
chapter has suffered serious disturbance, and little help can be
gained from the ancient versions. The obscurities are not,
however, such as to make uncertain the general bearing of
the verses.

By oppression...away: i.e. his removal, though under a form
of justice, was virtually an act of tyranny. The rendering of the
marg., '*From* oppression...,' suggests that death released him
from the cruelty of his foes, but does not seem appropriate to
the words which follow. A proposed translation 'Excluded
from judgement...' yields an excellent sense but requires a small
change in the text.

as for...considered: this translation is possible but far from
natural. The A.V. 'Who shall declare his generation?' is
certainly incorrect, and other suggested renderings are not very
convincing, e.g. (1) 'Who inquires after his dwelling place?'
(2) 'Who considered his way (or 'fate')?'

living? for the transgression of my people was he stricken.
9 And they made his grave with the wicked, and with the
rich in his death; although he had done no violence,
neither was any deceit in his mouth.

---

of my people: the isolated introduction of the pron. in
1st pers. sing. is startling, and, if correct, would be fatal to the
view that the heathen are the speakers in this chapter, *vv.* 1–9.
It would further constitute a serious obstacle to the opinion
that the Servant is the nation of Israel, in any ordinary accepta-
tion of the term; for surely to say bluntly that Israel (the
Servant) is smitten for Israel would be far-fetched. At any rate
one could hardly maintain more than that the Servant might
personify a section of Israel or an ideal Israel not actually
coextensive with the historic people. If the 1st pers. 'my' is
retained, we would have to suppose that either Yahwe or the
Servant is the speaker, but there are weighty objections to both
suppositions. In view of this perplexity and the unsatisfactory
state of the text throughout these closing verses, no stress can be
laid on this solitary use of the 1st pers. It is legitimate to adopt
an easy emendation; read 'for our transgressions.'

was he stricken: lit. 'a stroke was upon them'—although
'upon him' is just possible as a rendering. It is generally
agreed that we should read, following the LXX and adding
only one letter in the Heb., 'he was smitten unto death.'
Whether we are to understand his death as due to his disease
or directly to the violence and injustice of his human foes is not
clear.

9. they made: render 'his grave was made....'

with the rich: this reading is possible, but a synonym for
'wicked' in the parallel clause is to be expected. Simple
emendations yield words meaning (1) 'oppressors,' (2) 'evil-
doers.'

in his death: lit. 'in his deaths.' The plural admits of no
plausible explanation; read, with the LXX, the sing. 'death.'
An alternative reading 'his high-place' has some MSS support
and some scholars prefer to adopt it, rendering 'his sepulchral
mound.' Unfortunately it is doubtful if the word can bear that
special meaning.

although...mouth: absolute sinlessness is not directly pre-
dicated of the Servant either here or in the other Songs.
Nevertheless his unfailing gentleness, his unwavering self-sacrifice
in vicarious suffering, and his faithfulness even unto death are
the essential proof of an innocent character.

10–12.   *The final glory of the Servant.*

Yet it pleased the LORD to bruise him ; he hath put 10
him to grief : when thou shalt make his soul an offering
for sin, he shall see *his* seed, he shall prolong his days,

10–12. In these concluding verses the texts of the LXX and
the Heb. differ greatly from one another, and both are full of
obscurity. It is possible, however, to rely upon the correctness
of the affirmation that the Servant, through the power of God,
is about to experience a resurrection to a new and glorious
existence, in which he will witness the attainment of his
beneficent ideal for mankind.

10.   Yet it...grief : a difficult clause. The Heb. word which
is rendered 'he hath put him to grief' (or marg. 'subjected him
to disease') undoubtedly requires to be emended : 'incurably'
is a possible correction. Even so the phrase 'Yahwe was
pleased to bruise (better 'crush') him' is open to grave suspicion.
It reads like a reassertion of the opinion which the speakers in
this chapter tell us they once entertained (*v.* 4) but now have
realised to be false. As such, the sentiment would seem to be
out of place at this point. The LXX implies readings which
would entirely alter the tone of the verse : (1) 'Yahwe was
pleased with His Servant,' or (2) 'Yahwe was pleased to cleanse
(justify) him from disease.'

when thou...sin : again a most obscure phrase. The sudden
introduction of the 2nd pers. 'thou'—addressed apparently to
Yahwe—is inexplicable, except on the supposition that the
prophet is speaking, and there are weighty objections to that
view. Even if the 3rd pers. 'he' be read, the hypothetical
and future character of the statement seems very strange, after
the explicit declaration (*vv.* 7–9) that the Servant has already
laid down his life. A possible alternative is to regard 'soul'
as the subj., translating 'When his soul shall make an offering-
for-sin' (lit. 'a guilt-offering,' by which is signified a sacrifice
presented as a compensation for an infringement of the rights of
others, Lev. v. 14 ff.). An ingenious emendation gives the sense
'though his soul should take on itself the guilt'; but none of
these renderings inspires confidence.

he shall see...days : however impossible it may be to determine
the details, it is practically certain that this verse asserts the
resurrection of the Servant from the death to which he has
submitted.   This fact constitutes an argument against proposals
to identify the Servant with any individual man, since the hope
of personal immortality or resurrection finds expression only in
the latest stage of O.T. thought.

and the pleasure of the LORD shall prosper in his hand.
11 He shall see of the travail of his soul, *and* shall be
satisfied : by his knowledge shall my righteous servant
12 justify many : and he shall bear their iniquities.   Therefore will I divide him a portion with the great, and he
shall divide the spoil with the strong ; because he poured
out his soul unto death, and was numbered with the transgressors : yet he bare the sin of many, and made inter-
cession for the transgressors.

---

11.   He shall see...satisfied : lit. 'Free from (or 'after')
the travail of his soul he shall see with satisfaction.' Metrically
the clause is deficient, and the reading of the LXX is worth
notice: 'And it pleased Yahwe to deliver him (last line of *v.* 10)
from the trouble of his soul, to cause him to see light and to
satisfy him.'

by his knowledge: i.e. knowledge of the mind and will of
God, religious insight.

my righteous servant: omit 'righteous.' As the text stands
the confession of the Gentiles must be taken to end with *v.* 9
or 10, the use of 'my' here and of 'I' in *v.* 12ª implying that
Yahwe is the speaker in these concluding verses.   It is true that
the 'I' in *v.* 12ª is open to question and could easily be altered
to the 3rd pers., whilst 'my' here may be changed to 'his' by
a very small correction; and in that case there would be no
need to assume a change of speaker.   But religious and literary
feeling unite in supporting the likelihood that, as the passage
began with the words of Yahwe (lii. 13–15), so it should
conclude with His pronouncement of the verdict vindicating
His Servant.

iniquities : better 'penalties,' cp. *v.* 4.

12.   Therefore...strong : in detail we must regard the language
as metaphorical, for the patient martyr will surely not turn into
a ruthless conqueror bent on the plunder of his beaten foes.
Yet it is no doubt literal to this extent that the moral exaltation
will be accompanied by political supremacy, a supremacy, however, which is conceived as taking its rise in the joyful and
voluntary recognition by the Gentiles of the Servant's religious
preeminence.

will I divide: LXX 'he shall receive.'

was numbered: cp. Mark xv. 28; Luke xxii. 37.

yet...transgressors : better 'yet he bare the punishment....'
The words summarise the reality behind the appearance; they
show the meaning of the Servant's death and the cause of his glory.

liv. *Redeemed Jerusalem.*
1-10. *The felicity of Zion.*

Sing, O barren, thou that didst not bear ; break forth **54**
into singing, and cry aloud, thou that didst not travail
with child : for more are the children of the desolate
than the children of the married wife, saith the LORD.
Enlarge the place of thy tent, and let them stretch forth 2
the curtains of thine habitations ; spare not : lengthen
thy cords, and strengthen thy stakes. For thou shalt 3
spread abroad on the right hand and on the left ; and
thy seed shall possess the nations, and make the desolate
cities to be inhabited. Fear not ; for thou shalt not be 4
ashamed : neither be thou confounded ; for thou shalt not
be put to shame : for thou shalt forget the shame of thy
youth, and the reproach of thy widowhood shalt thou
remember no more. For thy Maker is thine husband ; 5
the LORD of hosts is his name : and the Holy One of

---

liv. Apart from the two Servant-songs (l. 4–9 ; lii. 13–liii. 12),
the theme of the prophecy from xlix. 14 has been the imminent
consolation of Zion and its inhabitants. Here this expectation
is concluded in a paean of rejoicing. In *vv.* 1–10 Zion in the
hour of deliverance is presented under the figure of a wife
reunited to her husband and her children and assured that
everlasting tenderness will be her portion. In *vv.* 11–17 the
glory and security of the restored city are depicted in glowing
language.

1. for more...wife : i.e. the inhabitants of the restored city
will surpass in number those which she had in the most prosperous
days before the Exile.

2. Enlarge...stakes : for the metaphoric use of 'tent' to
denote a city cp. xxxiii. 20 ; and for the thought that the area
of Zion will need enlargement to accommodate its people
cp. xlix. 18–21.

4. shame...youth : probably, the bondage in Egypt.

reproach...widowhood : i.e. the exilic period, when Yahwe
temporarily withdrew from Zion ; for, as appears from l. 1, the
separation was not of an absolute nature. Note that ' widowhood' has a wider significance than in English, being used here
to denote a woman abandoned by her husband.

Israel is thy redeemer; the God of the whole earth shall
6 he be called. For the LORD hath called thee as a wife
forsaken and grieved in spirit, even a wife of youth, when
7 she is cast off, saith thy God. For a small moment have
I forsaken thee; but with great mercies will I gather thee.
8 In overflowing wrath I hid my face from thee for a
moment; but with everlasting kindness will I have mercy
9 on thee, saith the LORD thy redeemer. For this is *as*
the waters of Noah unto me: for as I have sworn that
the waters of Noah should no more go over the earth, so
have I sworn that I would not be wroth with thee, nor
10 rebuke thee. For the mountains shall depart, and the
hills be removed; but my kindness shall not depart from
thee, neither shall my covenant of peace be removed,
saith the LORD that hath mercy on thee.

11–17.   The splendour and safety of Zion.

11   O thou afflicted, tossed with tempest, and not comforted, behold, I will set thy stones in fair colours, and lay

---

6.   even a wife...off: render 'and a wife of youth—can she
be rejected (i.e. permanently abandoned)?'

8.   To the average Israelite the Exile had seemed intermin-
ably long; to the faith of the prophet it is as a shadow veiling
for a moment the sunshine of God's eternal mercy.

9.   For this...Noah: read ' For as the days of Noah is this
(the renewed covenant) unto me.' The present promise is as
eternal as that of which the rainbow was made for Noah the
everlasting token (Gen. ix. 12 ff.).

10.   For the mountains: better 'Though.' The new covenant
is further confirmed by the might of the eternal hills.

11–17.   A description of the new Jerusalem, and—in conclusion—an assertion of its inviolable security, cp. Rev. xxi.
18–21.

11.   in fair colours: lit. 'in antimony,' a pigment customarily
used by women for darkening the eyelids to show off by
contrast the sparkle of the eyes. Presumably therefore the
metaphor here implies that the stones of the walls are to be
set with dark cement in order to set off their dazzling white-
ness. The context, however, favours an easy emendation, 'with
emeralds' (or 'carbuncles').

thy foundations with sapphires. And I will make thy 12
pinnacles of rubies, and thy gates of carbuncles, and all
thy border of pleasant stones. And all thy children shall 13
be taught of the LORD; and great shall be the peace of
thy children. In righteousness shalt thou be established: 14
thou shalt be far from oppression, for thou shalt not fear;
and from terror, for it shall not come near thee. Behold, 15
they may gather together, but not by me: whosoever shall
gather together against thee shall fall because of thee.
Behold, I have created the smith that bloweth the fire of 16
coals, and bringeth forth a weapon for his work; and I
have created the waster to destroy. No weapon that is 17
formed against thee shall prosper; and every tongue that
shall rise against thee in judgement thou shalt condemn.

---

lay thy foundations: read simply 'and thy foundations.'

12. thy border: probably not the boundary of the land, but
the external wall of the city.

13, 14. The inward conditions shall match the outward
splendour.

13. all thy...Lord: cp. the famous utterance in Jer. xxxi. 34,
'And they shall teach no more every man his neighbour...saying,
Know the Lord; for they shall all know me from the least of them
unto the greatest.' Owing to the repetition of the word 'children,'
some would substitute for it at the beginning of the verse, 'thy
builders.' The change in Heb. would be insignificant.

14. In righteousness: either by the character of the citizens,
or by the victory, i.e. the firm establishment, of the State.

15. Translate 'If they stir up strife, it is not of me (i.e. at
my bidding). Whoever stirs up strife with thee shall fall over
thee' (i.e. shatter themselves against thee), cp. viii. 14 f. The
doctrine of Zion as the inviolable city, which Isaiah first preached,
which Jeremiah later denounced when misconceived by the people,
and which finally collapsed in the stern fact of Jerusalem's
downfall, is now revived in all its comforting assurance.

16. God has created both the makers and the wielders of
the weapons of war. Zion therefore need feel no fear, if God
watches over its safety.

for his work: better, as marg., 'for its work,' i.e. for its
special function.

17. every tongue: Zion need not fear even malicious talk.
She shall be able to prove the slanders false.

This is the heritage of the servants of the LORD, and
their righteousness which is of me, saith the LORD.

lv. *An appeal to individuals to participate in the
new Covenant.*

1–5. *Its blessings freely offered.*

55 Ho, every one that thirsteth, come ye to the waters,
and he that hath no money; come ye, buy, and eat; yea,
come, buy wine and milk without money and without
2 price.   Wherefore do ye spend money for that which is
not bread? and your labour for that which satisfieth not?
hearken diligently unto me, and eat ye that which is good,
3 and let your soul delight itself in fatness.   Incline your
ear, and come unto me; hear, and your soul shall live:

This: the peace and prosperity just described.

servants: i.e. 'worshippers'; but possibly the word here has
more than its customary meaning, and is intended as a link
with the Servant-songs. The prophet perhaps wishes to suggest
that in the ideal city each individual shall reproduce the features
of that Ideal Servant who has been portrayed in the four Songs.

righteousness: 'their state of victorious bliss.'

lv. The proclamation of Zion's felicity being concluded,
the prophet invites all men freely to share in the blessings of
the new era: only so will they find peace unto their souls
(*vv.* 1–5). One cannot fail to perceive a note of wistfulness in
the appeal, suggestive of the dread of an unspeakable disappointment. Some, perhaps many, even in Israel have shown
signs of remaining indifferent to the Divine promise (*vv.* 6, 7);
as though after all they would choose the flesh-pots of an alien
home rather than the mercies of their gracious pardoning God
(*vv.* 8–13).

1. buy wine...price: or 'buy corn without money, and without
price wine and milk.' The language is of course chiefly metaphorical, yet not exclusively so, for the blessings of peace and
plenty were naturally expected as a feature of the new age.

2. not bread: the material luxuries of their alien homes,
however plentiful, will leave the true spiritual life of the nation
without sustenance. Moreover for these ultimately worthless
possessions they have to spend their strength, whereas the in-
estimable advantages which God offers can be obtained simply
by obedience to His call.

labour: read 'earnings.'

and I will make an everlasting covenant with you, even
the sure mercies of David.　Behold, I have given him 4
for a witness to the peoples, a leader and commander to
the peoples.　Behold, thou shalt call a nation that thou 5
knowest not, and a nation that knew not thee shall run
unto thee, because of the LORD thy God, and for the
Holy One of Israel ; for he hath glorified thee.

6-13. A call to penitence, and an assurance of blessing.

Seek ye the LORD while he may be found, call ye upon 6

---

fatness: i.e. the highest blessings, especially spiritual well-
being, cp. xxv. 6.　Contrast Ps. cvi. 15, 'And He gave them
their request but sent leanness into their souls.'

3.　everlasting covenant: Israel's hope finds expression in the
longing that the Covenant relationship with its God, abrogated
at the Exile, may some day by His mercy be renewed, cp.
Jer. xxxi. 27-34 ; Ezek. xxxiv. 23 ff.　Unlike the first, the new
Covenant shall be eternal.

even...David: the promise, made under the old Covenant,
that the Davidic kingdom would never cease (2 Sam. vii. 8-16;
Ps. xviii. 50) is to be realised in the new era of Divine favour
and prosperity.

4.　him: a difficult verse. Does the pron. refer to the historic
David or to some future Davidic King who is to reign in the
coming era?　The former is somewhat easier grammatically,
the latter preferable from the point of view of exposition; but
both interpretations are open to serious objections.　If we read
'I have given thee' (a change of one letter in Heb.) the verse
would be in harmony with the succeeding verse as well as with
the general conceptions of the prophecy.

5.　The heathen peoples will flock to Jerusalem that they
may acknowledge Yahwe as the true and only God and share
the blessings of His people.

6-13.　'Repent, for the Kingdom of God is at hand'; and
know that the penitent will not be refused, since God is
merciful beyond all human thought.　He wills the restoration
of all mankind to joy, peace, and prosperity, and He will not
rest until His holy purpose is achieved.

6.　while...found: cp. xlix. 8.　Whilst here the offer of God's
mercy is presented as a fleeting opportunity, in many passages
the restoration of Israel seems to have been promised uncon-
ditionally, as an inevitable outcome of God's purpose (cp. *v.* 11).

7 him while he is near : let the wicked forsake his way, and
the unrighteous man his thoughts : and let him return
unto the LORD, and he will have mercy upon him ; and
8 to our God, for he will abundantly pardon. For my
thoughts are not your thoughts, neither are your ways
9 my ways, saith the LORD. For as the heavens are higher
than the earth, so are my ways higher than your ways,
10 and my thoughts than your thoughts. For as the rain
cometh down and the snow from heaven, and returneth
not thither, but watereth the earth, and maketh it bring
forth and bud, and giveth seed to the sower and bread to
11 the eater; so shall my word be that goeth forth out of
my mouth : it shall not return unto me void, but it shall
accomplish that which I please, and it shall prosper in
12 the thing whereto I sent it. For ye shall go out with joy,
and be led forth with peace : the mountains and the hills
shall break forth before you into singing, and all the trees
13 of the field shall clap their hands. Instead of the thorn
shall come up the fir tree, and instead of the brier shall
come up the myrtle tree : and it shall be to the LORD for
a name, for an everlasting sign that shall not be cut off.

If this fact be a paradox, it is only the abiding paradox of all
religious appeal: God's love is eternal, yet the present chance
of accepting it is transient, and cannot be refused without
permanent loss.

8, 9. Human thought is so swift to despair of the possibility
of salvation. With its pettiness, contrast the sublimity of the
Divine thought, which transcends all human hopes in its willingness to pardon and in its power to restore.

10, 11. An exquisite conception of the relation between God
and man. As falling rain must inevitably reach the earth and
fulfil its part in the growth of vegetation, so the spirit of God
ceaselessly works to fructify the heart of man. The earth may
be too barren to respond to the rain and bear fruit, and man
likewise may resist God's influence; but he cannot deny His love.

12. led forth : by God, cp. xlii. 16; xlviii. 21; xlix. 10; lii. 12.

13. for a name...sign: as the rainbow was made the visible
token of the first Covenant, so the sign of the second shall be the
loveliness of the blossoming desert.

lvi.–lxvi.   ORACLES OF MENACE TO THE WICKED AND OF
ENCOURAGEMENT FOR THE GODLY

lvi. 1–8.   *Confirmation to Proselytes and Eunuchs
of the privileges of the Temple worship.*

Thus saith the LORD, Keep ye judgement, and do **56**
righteousness : for my salvation is near to come, and my
righteousness to be revealed. Blessed is the man that 2

---

lvi.–lxvi. See Introd. p. xxi f.

lvi. 1–8. This section shows no necessary connection with the
preceding chapters, or with the verses which immediately follow ;
but it has affinities with the tone and aspiration of various passages
in chs. lvii. ff. After an exhortation to moral behaviour and proper
observance of religious ceremony (*vv.* 1, 2), an assurance is given
to eunuchs and to alien residents that they will not be debarred
from the privileges of worshipping Yahwe in the Temple and so
sharing in the blessings of Israel's covenant (*vv.* 3–8). The
circumstances and problems here contemplated are separated
from the situation outlined in II Isaiah by a change of outlook
requiring the lapse of many years. Thus the passage implies
the existence of the Temple (*vv.* 5, 7), and of an established
Jewish community for whom a settled religious ritual has become
a peculiar privilege. Considerable time must be allowed for the
growth of the exclusive spirit here condemned as unworthy of
the universality of Israel's faith. The language of *v.* 8, and the
presence of eunuchs in sufficient numbers to raise an important
issue, may be taken as proof that a partial return from exile has
taken place, although a greater and general restoration is still
hoped for. Altogether it seems most probable that the prophecy
is addressed to the post-exilic community in Jerusalem.

1. for my...revealed : 'Repent, for the Kingdom of God is
at hand,' cp. xlvi. 13 ; lv. 6. The expectation that salvation is
close at hand figures prominently in chs. lvi. ff. just as in chs.
xl.–lv. This fact cannot, however, be pressed into service as an
argument for identity of authorship or even approximation of
date between the two sections, for the same hope is entertained
in the post-exilic writers Haggai, Zechariah, and Malachi. The
actual facts of the Return and the rebuilding of the Temple
formed so faint a realisation of II Isaiah's golden visions, that
the expectation of a far more glorious and general restoration
continued to be an ardent hope among the prophets of the
new community.

righteousness : in the first part of the verse the word obviously
stands for moral conduct, obedience to the precepts of God

doeth this, and the son of man that holdeth fast by it ;
that keepeth the sabbath from profaning it, and keepeth
3 his hand from doing any evil. Neither let the stranger,
that hath joined himself to the LORD, speak, saying, The
LORD will surely separate me from his people : neither
4 let the eunuch say, Behold, I am a dry tree. For thus
saith the LORD of the eunuchs that keep my sabbaths,
and choose the things that please me, and hold fast by
5 my covenant : Unto them will I give in mine house and

(cp. lviii. 2); at the end of the verse it is equivalent to 'success,'
the result of His unalterable purpose of redemption.

2. man ∥ son of man: the terms are practically synonymous,
denoting any individual human being.

the sabbath: for this writer, here and again in lviii. 13 (where
see note), sincere observance of the Sabbath law assumes a
degree of importance foreign to II Isaiah, who does not refer
to the subject at all.   The ancient Israelite institution of the
Sabbath rest increased in importance during the exilic period,
when the observance of this day, together with the rite of
circumcision, became the chief external tokens of adherence to
the Jewish faith (cp. Ezek. xx. 12).   But, since neither II Isaiah,
Haggai, Zechariah, nor even Malachi refers to the institution, it
is practically certain that it did not become a burning question
until about the period of Nehemiah.   The stress here laid on
the subject is therefore important evidence as to the date.

3. the stranger...people: since the aliens referred to here
have been admitted to association in the worship of Israel,
the prophet is evidently not objecting to laws regulating
and restricting the incorporation of foreigners as members of
the nation, see e.g. Deut. xxiii. 3–8.   We must infer that there
was a growing spirit of arrogance and intolerance on the part of
certain Jews against the proselytes resident in their midst.   The
prophet wishes to protest against the injustice of seeking to
deprive them of rights already acquired.   When we contrast
xliv. 5, where the willing adherence of alien proselytes is joyfully anticipated, with the rigidly exclusive attitude adopted by
Nehemiah (Neh. ix. 2, xiii. 1–3), it seems reasonable to suppose
that the present passage belongs to an intermediate date.

eunuch: such persons were excluded from the congregation of
Yahwe by the Deuteronomic code.   The prophet's protest is
perhaps directed against the application of the rule to persons
who had suffered involuntary mutilation.

4. of: i.e. 'with regard to.'

within my walls a memorial and a name better than of
sons and of daughters; I will give them an everlasting
name, that shall not be cut off. Also the strangers, that 6
join themselves to the LORD, to minister unto him, and to
love the name of the LORD, to be his servants, every one
that keepeth the sabbath from profaning it, and holdeth
fast by my covenant; even them will I bring to my holy 7
mountain, and make them joyful in my house of prayer;
their burnt offerings and their sacrifices shall be accepted
upon mine altar: for mine house shall be called an house
of prayer for all peoples. The Lord GOD which gathereth 8
the outcasts of Israel saith, Yet will I gather *others* to
him, beside his own that are gathered.

---

5. a memorial...cut off: i.e. the names of these persons
will be inscribed on a memorial (lit. 'hand'—a tablet or pillar)
in the Temple. Their name will share the permanence of the
shrine itself, and will thus be perpetuated with even greater
security than by a line of descendants, which might become
extinct.

6. to minister: i.e. to 'honour,' 'worship'; for the word in
this connection can hardly refer, as it does elsewhere in the
O.T., to the performance of priestly functions.

7. Even aliens, who observe the above conditions, shall have
free access to the Temple ministrations.

make them joyful: i.e. permit them to 'rejoice before the
Lord'—the technical Deuteronomic phrase for participation in
the religious festivals.

mine house...prayer: quoted in Mark xi. 17; Matt. xxi. 13;
Luke xix. 46.

for all peoples: this is the essential teaching of the whole
section. The writer has taken to heart the religious universalism
so finely expressed in II Isaiah, esp. in the Servant-songs:
to him the Jerusalem Temple is the House of the God of the
whole earth and must therefore be open for prayer not only to
the Jews but also equally to all genuine religious aspirants of
whatever race.

8. outcasts: rather 'dispersed.'

Yet will...gathered: lit. 'I will further gather to him, to his
gathered ones.' The language plainly suggests that a partial
return from exile has taken place; but that a further 'gathering'
is to be expected, a gathering which will include not simply
Israelites of the Dispersion but men of all nations.

lvi. 9–lvii. 21. *Denunciations of unfaithful rulers and
of idolaters, followed by encouragement for the righteous.*

lvi. 9–lvii. 2. *The corrupt rulers of Israel.*

9   All ye beasts of the field, come to devour, *yea*, all ye
10 beasts in the forest.   His watchmen are blind, they are
all without knowledge; they are all dumb dogs, they

---

lvi. 9–lvii. 21. This section falls into three parts : (1) an ex-
posure of the defenceless position of the community owing to the
folly, greed, and sensuality of its unscrupulous rulers, who heedlessly permit the destruction of its noblest members (lvi. 9–lvii. 2);
(2) a fiery invective against a party guilty of degraded paganism
(lvii. 3–13); (3) a message of reassurance addressed to the
humble and contrite people of God (lvii. 14–21).   Whether
these three passages, especially the last, stood originally in juxta-
position and were intended to form a whole must remain an
open question.   That the first two parts at least cannot be
assigned to any writer of the exilic period appears certain not
only from the clear implication that at this period Israel is
under the guidance of its own leaders and open to attack in
consequence of their neglect of duty, but also from the
Palestinian features of the idolatries described.   An explanation of these features used to be sought in the supposition
that II Isaiah had, as a warning against the recrudescence of
idolatry, here incorporated the document of a pre-exilic writer
denouncing the abuses current (say) in the reign of Manasseh.
The improbability of this theory is obvious, and, when the
section is considered in conjunction with the features presented
in the succeeding chapters, it can hardly be doubted that the
reference is to the dangers, material and moral, which attended
the existence of the post-exilic community.   The picture is
suitable to the condition of affairs *c.* 460 B.C., i.e. shortly before
the advent of Ezra and Nehemiah, cp. Mal. ii. 11, iii. 5;
Neh. v. 2–11.

lvi. 9–lvii. 2. A call to the wild animals (heathen nations) to
come and prey upon Israel, which is left defenceless through
the vices of its rulers.

9.   beasts of the field ‖ forest: i.e. any people hostile to
Israel.   Although Judaea was nominally part of the Persian
Empire in the 6th cent., it was exposed to the petty but
galling assaults of marauding neighbours (cp. Zech. viii. 10;
Neh. iv. 8 f.).

10.   watchmen...dumb dogs : Israel, the flock, ought to be
securely guarded by its priests and prophets (the watchdogs),
and by its civil rulers (the shepherds, *v.* 11).   But the leaders

cannot bark ; dreaming, lying down, loving to slumber.
Yea, the dogs are greedy, they can never have enough ; 11
and these are shepherds that cannot understand : they
have all turned to their own way, each one to his gain,
from every quarter.   Come ye, *say they*, I will fetch wine, 12
and we will fill ourselves with strong drink ; and to-morrow
shall be as this day, *a day* great beyond measure.

The righteous perisheth, and no man layeth it to **57**
heart ; and merciful men are taken away, none considering
that the righteous is taken away from the evil *to come.*

---

fail to perceive the result of the ethical and religious corruption
of the nation; and do not warn the people of the peril of
their degenerate state.

11. the dogs are greedy: the mischief is not simply a lazy
neglect of duty.   There is unscrupulous and insatiable self-
seeking.

these are shepherds: better, with a small change of
text, 'and these, the shepherds,' i.e. the civil authorities, the
actual rulers of the State, cp. Zech. xi. 5.   The records of
Nehemiah show all too clearly that the history of the restored
community added only another chapter to the old miserable tale
of Israel's economic and moral degradation through the ruthless
misuse by the rich of their power over their poorer countrymen.

from every quarter: render 'one and all'; but the word should
probably be deleted.

12.   To their inhuman greed, the nobles and rulers add the
vices of intemperate feasting.

to-morrow...as this day: the supreme miscalculation.   Human
history does not stand still, and each human life is either rising
or descending in the scale of being.

lvii. 1.   The exploitation of the nation is costing it dear.
The strength of its life is being sapped through the loss of its
righteous citizens, who can safely be murdered whilst the ruling
classes remain callously indifferent to their fate.

merciful men: 'men of piety' (Heb. **hesed**).   The term meets
us in the title 'Ḥasidim' applied to the sorely persecuted godly
party in the days of the Maccabees (*c.* 168 B.C.).   It is possible
that these two verses, or this particular phrase, were added in
that period.

none...righteous: better, as LXX, 'and none regardeth ; for
the righteous....'

is taken...evil: there is no occasion to supply, as R.V. text,
the words 'to come.'   The evil is the existing state of oppression

2 He entereth into peace ; they rest in their beds, each one
that walketh in his uprightness.

3–13 a. *A denunciation of certain gross idolaters.*

3 But draw near hither, ye sons of the sorceress, the
4 seed of the adulterer and the whore. Against whom do
ye sport yourselves? against whom make ye a wide mouth,
and draw out the tongue? are ye not children of trans-
5 gression, a seed of falsehood, ye that inflame yourselves
among the oaks, under every green tree ; that slay the
children in the valleys, under the clefts of the rocks?
6 Among the smooth *stones* of the valley is thy portion ;

---

and injustice.   Render 'the righteous is swept away before the
evil,' or '...through the iniquity' (of the time).

2.   The 'peace' and 'rest' are those of death and the underworld of Sheol. If such language can be used of the cheerless
shadow-life of Sheol, as it was conceived at this period, how
terrible must be the tumult of wickedness in the Jewish community!

3–13 a.   The prophet now turns to direct an invective against
certain persons who have devoted themselves to loathsome
idolatries (*vv.* 3–10). God has been patient, but the hour of
their overthrow is at hand, when they will discover the futility
of the rites in which they have put their trust (*vv.* 11–13ª).   In
many details of text the passage is obscure; but it is perfectly
clear from the scenery referred to in *vv.* 5, 6, and from the
nature of the rites in question, that the section is Palestinian.
It is natural to assign the passage to post-exilic times, and to
regard it as an attack upon the semi-pagan population of
Samaria and Judaea, or upon a party in Jerusalem favourable
to a nominal worship of Yahwe combined with acceptance of
the foul Canaanite deities.

3.   draw...hither: to hear your doom.   The metaphor of the
verse may have reference either to the idolatrous practices of
the accused persons, or to a mixed origin—half Hebrew, half
foreign.

5.   oaks: or 'terebinths,' cp. i. 29; lxi. 3.   The reference
may be to actual tree-worship, which persists to this day in
Palestine, or, more probably, to the sacred trees as the scene of
the revels with which the god was honoured.

6.   To the gods of the trees are added the gods of the
torrent valleys.   The worship of these deities was associated

they, they are thy lot : even to them hast thou poured a
drink offering, thou hast offered an oblation.   Shall I be
appeased for these things?   Upon a high and lofty 7
mountain hast thou set thy bed : thither also wentest thou
up to offer sacrifice.   And behind the doors and the posts 8
hast thou set up thy memorial : for thou hast discovered
thyself to another than me, and art gone up ; thou hast
enlarged thy bed, and made thee a covenant with them ;
thou lovedst their bed where thou sawest it.   And thou 9
wentest to the king with ointment, and didst increase thy

---

with the sacrifice of young children (*v.* 5), a practice not
uncommon among the nations of antiquity, cp. 2 Kings iii. 27 ;
Deut. xii. 31.   Possibly the story of the offering up of Isaac
(Gen. xxii.) implies that the custom once prevailed amongst the
earliest ancestors of Israel, and was eventually condemned by a
higher conception of the Divine will.   Child-sacrifice by fire
seems to have been regular in connection with Moloch-worship
(Jer. vii. 31, etc.), but it is possible that the ritual in this case
did not involve the child's death.

smooth (stones) : i.e. water-worn boulders, set up as objects of
worship.   The word, however, is selected because in Heb. it
yields an assonance with the word translated 'portion.'   Perhaps
therefore it should be interpreted not literally but metaphorically
'slippery ones,' i.e. false gods.   If so we must render 'among
the deceivers of the valley.'

portion : God is the true 'portion' (lot, inheritance) of
His people ; but these idolaters have placed their hopes on vain
illusions.

oblation : rather 'meal-offering.'   The drink-offering might
be of oil, or wine, or blood.

7.   To the gods of the torrent-beds they add the gods of the
hill-tops, cp. lxv. 7 ; Jer. ii. 20.   The use of the 2nd pers. sing.
(fem.) in this and the following verses means that the writer
addresses a personified community.

8.   The reference is to worship rendered to household deities.
By 'memorial' is meant some form of heathen emblem.   The
text, especially in the latter part of the verse, is obscure, and the
meaning uncertain.

9.   A difficult verse, best interpreted as a reference to the
adoption of foreign deities.

to the king : an allusion to political embassies is out of
keeping with the context.   The word 'king' (Heb. melek)
was applied as a title to many gods.   The term is really the same

perfumes, and didst send thine ambassadors far off, and
10 didst debase thyself even unto hell.   Thou wast wearied
with the length of thy way ; yet saidst thou not, There is
no hope: thou didst find a quickening of thy strength ;
11 therefore thou wast not faint.   And of whom hast thou
been afraid and in fear, that thou liest, and hast not
remembered me, nor laid it to thy heart? have not I held
my peace even of long time, and thou fearest me not?
12 I will declare thy righteousness ; and as for thy works,
13 they shall not profit thee.   When thou criest, let them
which thou hast gathered deliver thee ; but the wind shall

---

as the name 'Molech.'   If the verb 'journey,' be correct, the
verse must be taken to refer to pilgrimages to some foreign
shrine; but the LXX reads simply 'and thou didst anoint
thyself for Melek.'

didst debase...hell: lit. 'and didst make deep [thy sending]
even unto Sheol,' i.e. (apparently) didst consult deities of the
underworld.

10. a quickening...strength: lit. 'the life of thy hand,' an
obscure phrase.   The idolaters are wearied by their restless
search for help from the false gods, but are buoyed up by the
delusive hope that in yet another idol they may find what they
seek.

11. liest: rather 'art faithless.'   Clearly these idolaters are
persons who have had the opportunity of worshipping Yahwe.

have not I...not: or 'Is it not so?   I have been silent even
of long time so that thou fearest me not.'   For 'even of long
time,' the LXX has the preferable reading 'and hid mine eyes.'

12.   Their zeal in worship is ironically termed 'righteousness,'
a caricature of real spirituality.   Taken in conjunction with *v.* 11[a],
it seems clear that the passage refers to an attempt at propa-
gating a syncretistic religion, in which Yahwe was to be
worshipped along with Canaanite and foreign deities.   Whether
the advocates of this pseudo-faith had adherents among the
Jerusalem community or were confined to the mixed people
of Judaea and Samaria remains uncertain.   In any case the
prophet's burning indignation was doubtless justified, for an
unworthy or nominal adherent is always a more deadly foe to
any religion than an open opponent.

declare: i.e. expose its hypocritical nature.   At last God will
break His silence.

13. them...gathered: i.e., as marg., 'thy rabble of idols.'

take them, a breath shall carry them all away: but **he**
that putteth his trust in me shall possess the land, and
shall inherit my holy mountain.

14–21.   *Comfort for humble believers.*

And he shall say, Cast ye up, cast ye up, prepare the 14
way, take up the stumblingblock out of the way of my
people.

For thus saith the high and lofty One that inhabiteth 15
eternity, whose name is Holy: I dwell in the high and
holy place, with him also that is of a contrite and humble

---

but he...mountain: the clause forms a transition to the
ensuing section; but might equally be regarded as a suitable
close to the above section, see below.

14–21. So far as the sense is concerned, the present passage
might be regarded as the continuation of the two preceding
sections, the prophet here turning from the selfish rulers and
infidel rulers to contrast the peace and blessing which Yahwe,
the Omnipotent and Holy One, will assuredly bestow on all
contrite and humble souls, who are faithful to Him.   But a
marked alteration of style and a change of metre at this point
suggest that *vv.* 14 ff. were not originally connected with what
precedes.   The style is evidently based on that of II Isaiah,
but various details, as well as the general tone of the piece,
make it improbable that the passage is actually the work of that
prophet.

14. he shall say: the sense is obscure and awkward.   The
word may be regarded as a gloss intended to supply a subject
for the following imperative.

Cast ye up: the speaker is God, but it is doubtful whether the
command is addressed to angelic beings or to men.

prepare the way: obviously a reminiscence of xl. 3, although
the 'path' is to be interpreted less literally than in the earlier
passage, cp. lxii. 10.   Here, perhaps, it is meant chiefly as a
metaphor for the spiritual failings which the writer regards as
the real obstacle ('stumblingblock') to a general return of the
Dispersion.   Cp. Mark i. 3; John i. 23.

15. high and lofty: cp. ii. 12 ff.; vi. 1.

I dwell...place: rather 'I dwell in the height as the Holy
One.'   The verse is influenced both by the description of
I Isaiah's vision (ch. vi.) and by the thoughts of II Isaiah,
cp. ch. xl.

spirit, to revive the spirit of the humble, and to revive the
16 heart of the contrite ones. For I will not contend for
ever, neither will I be always wroth : for the spirit should
17 fail before me, and the souls which I have made. For
the iniquity of his covetousness was I wroth and smote
him, I hid *my face* and was wroth: and he went on fro-
18 wardly in the way of his heart. I have seen his ways, and
will heal him: I will lead him also, and restore comforts
19 unto him and to his mourners. I create the fruit of the

---

with him: the thought of the transcendent holiness of
God is incomplete apart from the equally vital belief that He
draws near to the broken and contrite heart. It is commonly
said that later O. T. theology placed God in a distant Heaven,
where He could be reached only through a host of intermediate
Beings. If such a feeling existed, it was a popular misconception, not shared by the spiritually minded Jews.

contrite: rather 'crushed': it does not imply remorse for sin.
The reference here is to the effects of the persecution and contempt
to which the pious section of the community has been subjected.
The writer has learnt that humble trust in the Divine purity and
power leads to peace and to faith in God's infinite compassion.

16. Recognition of the limit of human endurance is here
named as the reason why God will now show mercy. Contrast
this statement with (1) xl. 2, where the cause is said to be
the adequacy of the punishment already borne by Israel, and
(2) xlviii. 9, 11, where it is declared that further penalty is remitted by God, lest His Name should be brought into contempt
and be profaned by the heathen.

contend: i.e. chastise, punish.

17. For the...covetousness: or 'unjust gain.' Greed of
money seems to be singled out as the nation's besetting sin.
This may be taken as an indication that the passage is later
than the exilic period, and further that the persons here reproached are not the same as those guilty of the desperate
wickedness exposed in the previous section. It should, however, be noted that the LXX reads 'on account of his guilt
for a moment.'

frowardly: lit. ' turning away.' The evil conduct continues,
despite the Divine warning.

18. I...his ways: i.e. 'I have marked his wicked ways,'
connecting the words with the previous verse.

and...him: or 'yet I will heal him'—according to the view
taken of the preceding words (see previous note).

and...mourners: the clause should be united with the

lips: Peace, peace, to him that is far off and to him that is
near, saith the LORD; and I will heal him. But the 20
wicked are like the troubled sea; for it cannot rest, and
its waters cast up mire and dirt. There is no peace, saith 21
my God, to the wicked.

lviii. *The contrast between formal and genuine religion.*

Cry aloud, spare not, lift up thy voice like a trumpet, **58**
and declare unto my people their transgression, and to
the house of Jacob their sins. Yet they seek me daily, 2

---

following verse. Read 'And for his mourners I will create
the fruit of the lips,' i.e. restore praise and thanksgiving,
cp. Hos. xiv. 2.
   19. Peace, peace: i.e. profound peace: the word is governed
by 'I create.'
   far off ‖ near: the Jews in exile, and those in Jerusalem.
   and...him: an erroneous repetition from *v.* 18.
   21. The verse is found also in xlviii. 22, but is clearly in its
original setting here.
   lviii. The chapter sets forth the difference between the
religion of formalism and that which is born of genuine faith.
It opens with the command, which the prophet has received,
to expose the hypocrisy of the popular worship, and concludes
with an appeal to hallow the Sabbath day (*v.* 13), promising
that the blessings of salvation shall speedily reward a sincere
acceptance of true religion (*vv.* 8, 10–12, 14). Throughout,
the passage burns with spiritual passion. It is quite clear that
the community has set great store upon the diligent observance
of certain fasts, not yet realising the worthlessness of merely
formal religion. Such a situation suggests the post-exilic period,
for we know that a *system* of public fasts only developed during
the Exile (in commemoration of four disastrous days during the
last siege of Jerusalem) and that the question of their correct
observance agitated the mind of the restored community in the
days of Zechariah—see Zech. vii. 3 ff., viii. 19, passages which
afford most interesting parallels to the present chapter.
   1. declare...transgression: so also Mic. iii. 8. The false
prophet prophesies smooth things (1 Kings xxii. 13), but the
true prophet of Yahwe must declare the facts without fear or
favour.
   2. The nation lives blindly in the wilful delusion that zeal in
formal worship is all that is required.

and delight to know my ways: as a nation that did righteousness, and forsook not the ordinance of their God,
they ask of me righteous ordinances, they delight to draw
3 near unto God.   Wherefore have we fasted, *say they*, and
thou seest not? *wherefore* have we afflicted our soul, and
thou takest no knowledge? Behold, in the day of your
fast ye find *your own* pleasure, and exact all your labours.
4 Behold, ye fast for strife and contention, and to smite
with the fist of wickedness: ye fast not this day so as to
5 make your voice to be heard on high.   Is such the fast
that I have chosen? the day for a man to afflict his soul?
Is it to bow down his head as a rush, and to spread sackcloth and ashes under him? wilt thou call this a fast, and
6 an acceptable day to the LORD? Is not this the fast that

---

my ways: the meaning here must be, not the moral laws of
God (for these the people heedlessly violate) but simply the
ceremonial requirements of the Temple worship.

they ask...ordinances: i.e. concerning doubtful points of the
ritual, which they imagine is sufficient to make them 'righteous.'

3. Wherefore...no knowledge: the people had fondly hoped
that diligent attention to the ritual would secure the longed-for
blessings.   When they asked from Zechariah an explanation of
the delay in the coming of the blessings, he replied in much the
same fashion as this prophet, that the essential need is the
fulfilment of the moral obligation which God has taught
them through His servants, the prophets (Zech. viii. 19).

Behold...labours: the prophet in answer points to the fact
that those who observe so carefully the religious services are at
the same time careless of the lot of the labourers whom they
employ, allowing *them* no leisure to observe the fast lest their
profits should thereby be lessened.   The clause should be
translated 'Behold in the days of your fast ye find (opportunity
for) your own business and all your labourers ye drive.'

4.   Their fasts, instead of improving their characters, made
them irritable and quarrelsome, until at last there was open
brawling.   So long as this evil state of affairs continues, they
cannot expect their prayers to be heard and accepted by God.

5. to bow...under him: do they imagine that God will
be pleased with a multiplication of gestures or of physical
discomfort?

6, 7.   The true fast is an abstinence from injustice, and true

I have chosen? to loose the bonds of wickedness, to
undo the bands of the yoke, and to let the oppressed go
free, and that ye break every yoke? Is it not to deal thy 7
bread to the hungry, and that thou bring the poor that
are cast out to thy house? when thou seest the naked,
that thou cover him ; and that thou hide not thyself from
thine own flesh? Then shall thy light break forth as the 8
morning, and thy healing shall spring forth speedily: and
thy righteousness shall go before thee; the glory of the
LORD shall be thy rearward. Then shalt thou call, and 9
the LORD shall answer; thou shalt cry, and he shall say,
Here I am. If thou take away from the midst of thee
the yoke, the putting forth of the finger, and speaking
wickedly; and if thou draw out thy soul to the hungry, 10
and satisfy the afflicted soul ; then shall thy light rise in
darkness, and thine obscurity be as the noonday: and the 11

---

worship consists in the willing performance of social obligations ;
cp. James i. 27. Religion and social service are essentially
connected. See Matt. v. 7, vi. 12, xxv. 31-46.

6. bonds of wickedness: i.e. bonds wrongfully imposed.

oppressed: lit. 'the broken,' probably debtors who had been
forced to sell themselves to their creditors, cp. Neh. v. 5.

7. Compare Ezek. xviii. 7 f., and Neh. v. 17.

hide...flesh: i.e. do not make thyself inaccessible to needy
Israelites, thy brethren, who may come to implore assistance.

8. thy light: so also in *v.* 10, as the emblem of felicity,
cp. lx. 1, 3. To the merciful, God will manifest His mercy.

righteousness: the signs which show that Israel has won
Yahwe's approval, and is victorious, saved.

9. Then...I am: when the ethical conditions are fulfilled by
Israel, God will not fail to respond to prayer: contrast *v.* 3.

If thou...wickedly: the clause, which should be taken in
connection with *v.* 10, restates the hindrances which delay the
coming of salvation, whilst *v.* 10ᵃ repeats the ethical conditions,
fulfilment of which will certainly (*v.* 10ᵇ) result in the desired
blessings.

putting...finger: an offensive gesture expressive of contempt.

10. draw out thy soul: the expression in Heb. is far more
strained than the English suggests, and we should probably
read, on the basis of the LXX, 'and bestow thy bread on....'

LORD shall guide thee continually, and satisfy thy soul in
dry places, and make strong thy bones; and thou shalt
be like a watered garden, and like a spring of water,
12 whose waters fail not. And they that shall be of thee
shall build the old waste places: thou shalt raise up the
foundations of many generations; and thou shalt be called
The repairer of the breach, The restorer of paths to dwell
13 in. If thou turn away thy foot from the sabbath, from
doing thy pleasure on my holy day; and call the sabbath
a delight, *and* the holy of the LORD honourable; and
shalt honour it, not doing thine own ways, nor finding
14 thine own pleasure, nor speaking *thine own* words: then

---

11. guide thee: cp. lvii. 18.

make...bones: read rather 'and shall renew thy strength.'

a watered garden: i.e. Israel's prosperity shall be perennial.
For the metaphor, cp. xliv. 4; Jer. xxxi. 12.

12. they that...thee: the Heb. is peculiar; read perhaps
'thy sons.'

raise up...generations: i.e. thou shalt repair ruined buildings,
whose foundations have lain exposed for generations. Doubtless
the writer refers to the walls and houses of Jerusalem which
were destroyed in 597, and 586 B.C.; in which case the emphasis
laid on their ancient appearance suggests that the passage is
not earlier than the 5th century. The walls were rebuilt by
Nehemiah (*c.* 445 B.C.), on whom the ruinous appearance of the
city made a similarly deep impression (Neh. i. 3, ii. 2, 3).

paths to dwell in: i.e. paths which would facilitate settlement
in the land. It is perhaps better, changing one letter in the
text, to read 'ruins' instead of 'paths.' The vividness with
which the Hebrew mind could personify a nation makes the
use of the titles here applied to the community less strained
than it appears to be in the English.

13. turn...foot: the Sabbath is, so to speak, 'holy ground'
(cp. Exod. iii. 5).

from...pleasure: rather 'so as not to transact thy business.'

(and)...honourable: according to the Heb. text the phrase
'the holy of the Lord' must be regarded as a synonym for
'Sabbath.' The LXX reads (omitting the word 'honourable')
'and call the sabbath a delight and holy unto thy God.'

not doing...pleasure: cp. *v.* 3. For 'pleasure' translate, as
before, 'business.'

speaking...words: lit. 'a word.' They are not to disturb

shalt thou delight thyself in the LORD; and I will make thee to ride upon the high places of the earth; and I will feed thee with the heritage of Jacob thy father: for the mouth of the LORD hath spoken it.

lix.   *The miserable state of the Community, and the vengeance of Yahwe.*

1-8. *Sin is the real hindrance to salvation.*

Behold, the LORD'S hand is not shortened, that it can- **59** not save; neither his ear heavy, that it cannot hear: but **2** your iniquities have separated between you and your God, and your sins have hid his face from you, that he will not hear.   For your hands are defiled with blood, and your **3**

---

the services by private conversation, and so profane the worship.

14. delight thyself: better 'have delight,' i.e. in the felicitous conditions of life, which God will bestow.

ride...earth: Deut. xxxii. 13. God will enable Israel to surmount all obstacles and be supreme amongst the nations.

heritage...father: see Gen. xxvii. 27-29, xxviii. 13, 14; and cp. lxv. 9.

lix. The evil state of the community is explained in this chapter on practically the same principles as are set forth in ch. lviii., i.e. the complaint that God is unable or unwilling to save is mistaken. His power and His desire to bless are as great as ever, but cannot be manifested to those who live in moral degradation. The appalling sinfulness of the people (*vv.* 1-8) makes it impossible for God to assist them, and is therefore the true cause of their present desperate plight (*vv.* 9-15). Nevertheless God will not wait for the slow and uncertain movement of human justice, but will Himself take action and destroy His enemies, thus redeeming the true spiritual Zion (*vv.* 16-21). As in the previous chapter, the existence of a settled community responsible for the administration of justice is implied throughout, and must be regarded as a strong indication of post-exilic date. The unity of the chapter is questionable, see the notes to *v.* 5 and *v.* 15.

1. 2. Those who accuse God of lacking the power or the desire to save are utterly wrong. Nothing but the iniquity of Israel prevents the promised redemption.

2. have hid his face: i.e. have caused Him to refuse their petitions, and appear as though He did not hear them.

E.   7

fingers with iniquity ; your lips have spoken lies, your
4 tongue muttereth wickedness.   None sueth in righteousness, and none pleadeth in truth: they trust in vanity, and
speak lies; they conceive mischief, and bring forth
5 iniquity.   They hatch basilisks' eggs, and weave the
spider's web: he that eateth of their eggs dieth, and that
6 which is crushed breaketh out into a viper.   Their webs
shall not become garments, neither shall they cover themselves with their works : their works are works of iniquity,
7 and the act of violence is in their hands.   Their feet run
to evil, and they make haste to shed innocent blood:
their thoughts are thoughts of iniquity; desolation and
8 destruction are in their paths.   The way of peace they
know not; and there is no judgement in their goings:
they have made them crooked paths ; whosoever goeth
therein doth not know peace.

---

4.   Instead of redressing wrongs, the corrupt law-courts have
become the means by which the unscrupulous can attack and
plunder the victims of their malice or greed.

they trust, etc.: translate 'trusting...speaking...conceiving...
bringing.'

vanity: lit. 'chaos,' falsity.   The last clause of the verse
is found also in Job xv. 35.

5-8.   The verses may be an interpolation.   The change from
2nd to 3rd person is to be noted, the style resembles that of the
book of Proverbs, and the vehemence of the language is more
suitable in addressing a few peculiarly wicked persons than the
community in general.   Finally v. 9 connects quite as naturally
with v. 4 as v. 8.

5.   basilisks' eggs: basilisk: a deadly serpent, cp. xi. 8.
The point is that the plots hatched by these persons serve no
end save that of destruction.

he...dieth: either he who joins in the plot or he against
whom it is directed.

6.   The results of their schemes will be valueless even to
themselves.

7, 8.   Cp. Rom. iii. 15–17; Prov. i. 16.

8.   The way of peace : i.e. the manner of life which conduces
to peace.

judgement...goings: rather 'no justice in their tracks'
(habits of life).   The word 'tracks' is common in Proverbs.

*9-15 a. Acknowledgement of the national despair
and sinfulness.*

Therefore is judgement far from us, neither doth righteous- 9
ness overtake us: we look for light, but behold darkness;
for brightness, but we walk in obscurity. We grope for 10
the wall like the blind, yea, we grope as they that have no
eyes: we stumble at noonday as in the twilight; among
them that are lusty we are as dead men. We roar all 11
like bears, and mourn sore like doves: we look for judgement, but there is none; for salvation, but it is far off
from us. For our transgressions are multiplied before 12
thee, and our sins testify against us: for our transgressions
are with us, and as for our iniquities, we know them: in 13
transgressing and denying the LORD, and turning away

9-15 a. A graphic description of the national misery and
despair (*vv.* 9-11), followed by a confession of the sinfulness
which is their undoing. The prophet is the speaker, associating
himself with the community and expressing here the feelings
of those whose consciences are stirred by the terrible state of
affairs (*vv.* 12-15ᵃ). Remark the complete and pathetic contrast
with the high hopes of II Isaiah.

9. judgement...righteousness: i.e. vindication of the nation's
desires, salvation, prosperity; so also in *vv.* 11, 15.

10. A vivid metaphor to describe the nation's impotence and
insecurity.

at noonday: even when external circumstances are most
favourable, they remain in a condition of pitiable helplessness.

among...dead men: the Heb. is obscure.

11. roar: or 'growl.' The point, of course, lies not in any
note of anger in the sound, but in its suggestion of loneliness
and desolation, cp. 'the wolf's long howl on Oonalaska's shore.'
Similarly the cooing of doves is expressive of melancholy,
cp. xxxviii. 14, and Tennyson's line 'the moan of doves in
immemorial elms.'

12. are with us: i.e. are consciously realised; cp. Ps. li. 3.
The recognition of guilt clearly shows that the speakers are to
be distinguished from the hardened sinners of *vv.* 5-8.

13. A catalogue of sins. Probably the apostasy from Yahwe
is to be interpreted as referring less to actual idolatry than to
the moral denial involved in the practice of the social evils
enumerated above, *vv.* 3 ff.

from following our God, speaking oppression and revolt,
conceiving and uttering from the heart words of falsehood.

14 And judgement is turned away backward, and righteousness standeth afar off: for truth is fallen in the street, and
uprightness cannot enter.

*15 b–20.   The vengeance of Yahwe and deliverance
of the faithful.*

15 Yea, truth is lacking; and he that departeth from evil
maketh himself a prey: and the LORD saw it, and it dis-
16 pleased him that there was no judgement.   And he saw
that there was no man, and wondered that there was no
intercessor : therefore his own arm brought salvation unto
17 him ; and his righteousness, it upheld him.   And he put

---

14. Justice and righteousness (the moral qualities, not the
Divine vindication of Israel, as in *v.* 9) are here dramatically
personified.   They are depicted as eager to enter the city and
be present where the lawsuits were tried.   But they are unable.
to do so, whilst truth, the basis of civic virtue, lies prostrate on
the ground.

street: lit. 'broad place,' i.e. the open space, near the gates,
where the magistrates sat to administer justice, see Jer. v. 1;
Zech. viii. 16.

15. and he...prey: *not* to have a reputation as an evil-doer
is to single oneself out for persecution.

15 b–20. Humanly speaking, the situation appears hopeless,
for the wicked show no signs of penitence.   But God will
not tolerate their vice and cruelty to continue unchecked
(*v.* 15b).   Since no man is able to restrain them and turn them
from their iniquity, He Himself will interpose (*v.* 16).   Armed
with His holiness and power, He will deal justice : punishment
for His foes and redemption for His friends.

16. no man ‖ no intercessor: there appeared no champion
on behalf of truth and justice, none to rescue the down-trodden
saints.   Cp. the parallels in lii. 10, and lxiii. 1–6, where, however, the deliverance is from the tyranny of foreign nations.

therefore...upheld him : God will require no helpers besides
His own power ('arm') and character ('righteousness').   The
verbs, of course, do not refer to past time, but to a future
regarded as sure and potentially realised (prophetic perfect).

17. The panoply of God.   For the idea of Yahwe as a
warrior, see xlii. 13, xlix. 24 f., lii. 10; and cp. Eph. vi. 14.

on righteousness as a breastplate, and an helmet of salvation upon his head ; and he put on garments of vengeance
for clothing, and was clad with zeal as a cloke. According 18
to their deeds, accordingly he will repay, fury· to his
adversaries, recompence to his enemies ; to the islands
he will repay recompence. So shall they fear the name of 19
the LORD from the west, and his glory from the rising
of the sun : for he shall come as a rushing stream, which
the breath of the LORD driveth. And a redeemer shall 20
come to Zion, and unto them that turn from transgression
in Jacob, saith the LORD. And as for me, this is my 21
covenant with them, saith the LORD: my spirit that is
upon thee, and my words which I have put in thy mouth,
shall not depart out of thy mouth, nor out of the mouth

---

18. accordingly : omit. The text is uncertain.

to the islands : i.e. the heathen peoples of the seaboard
and islands : see the note on xl. 15. As the clause destroys the
balance of the verse and moreover is wanting in the LXX, it
may be a gloss, which has arisen through a misinterpretation of
v. 19.

19. The writer declares that the effects of the judgement will
be world-wide, inducing in all peoples the fear of the Lord;
but this is by no means the same thing as saying that the
judgement will be executed on all nations. The verse does not
demand, although it admits, the theory of a universal judgement.

for he...driveth : the coming of God in person has a
resistless force, like the rush of a great river pent in a narrow
channel and swept onward by the wind. The rendering of the
text is certainly superior to that of the marg. and A.V. 'when
the adversary shall come in like a flood, the spirit of the Lord
shall lift up a standard against him.'

20. And a...Zion : better 'But as a redeemer shall He come
to Zion.'

and unto...Jacob : the LXX is preferable: 'and shall turn
away iniquity from Jacob.'

21. my spirit...thy mouth : the statement might be applied
to the spiritual Israel; but if, as some think, the verse is an
addition, the reference will be to the community after it had
accepted the Law as promulgated in Ezra and Nehemiah's time.

upon thee : the change of person is due to the introduction of
direct speech.

of thy seed, nor out of the mouth of thy seed's seed,
saith the LORD, from henceforth and for ever.

60   Arise, shine ; for thy light is come, and the glory of the

---

nor...seed's seed : this clause makes it clear that the nation
is addressed, and not the prophet, since prophetic inspiration is
never regarded in the O.T. as a hereditary gift.

lx.–lxii.   These three chapters are distinguished both from
chs. lvi.–lix. and from chs. lxiii. ff. by characteristics of style and
outlook which clearly place them in a group by themselves.
They are a magnificent declaration of the glories Jerusalem will
enjoy in the era of Divine favour, which is on the point of being
revealed.   That resembles the historical standpoint of II Isaiah,
and, when further it is remarked that these chapters are
characterised throughout by the style which appears in chs. liv.,
lv., it would seem unwarrantable to ascribe this section to any
other author.   Two objections, however, require to be noticed.
(1) It is impossible to state any conclusive reason why, if these
three chapters are the work of II Isaiah, they should have been
sundered from chs. liv., lv., and placed where they now stand.
Still, it is true that such a displacement *might* have been made
either accidentally or deliberately in the process of collecting,
editing, or copying the prophecies.   (2) In lx. 7, 13, lxii. 8, 9,
words are used which, though not so definite as to be conclusive
(see notes lx. 7, lxii. 9), strongly suggest that the Temple was
already in existence.   If that view be correct, then either the
passage is a fifth century work, closely modelled on the style of
II Isaiah and composed about the same time as the preceding
chapters with the object of comforting the depressed and divided
community, or else it is the work of II Isaiah, but composed
after 516 B.C., when the Temple was rebuilt.   The first of these
alternatives is to be preferred.

lx.   The sequence of thought in chs. lx.–lxii. would be somewhat improved, if ch. lx. were transposed to follow ch. lxii.
The chapter is an address to Zion by Yahwe, who declares that
the moment of its redemption is come and sets forth the glories
of the era of Divine favour ; *vv.* 1–4 proclaim the dawn of this
new era, its effect on the Gentile world and on the Jewish exiles.

1.   Arise, shine : Zion has been, as it were, prostrate upon
the ground, and covered by the darkness of her afflictions
(cp. li. 17, lii. 2).

L<small>ORD</small> is risen upon thee. For, behold, darkness shall 2
cover the earth, and gross darkness the peoples : but the
L<small>ORD</small> shall arise upon thee, and his glory shall be seen .
upon thee. And nations shall come to thy light, and 3
kings to the brightness of thy rising. Lift up thine eyes 4
round about, and see : they all gather themselves together,
they come to thee : thy sons shall come from far, and thy
daughters shall be carried in the arms.

5-9. Zion enriched by the wealth of all nations.

Then thou shalt see and be lightened, and thine heart 5
shall tremble and be enlarged ; because the abundance of
the sea shall be turned unto thee, the wealth of the nations
shall come unto thee. The multitude of camels shall cover 6

---

thy light is come : the advent of the Divine favour resembles
the break of day : when the darkness passes, Jerusalem shines
forth conspicuous as its white buildings reflect the rays of the
sun. The tense 'is come' is prophetic perfect, i.e. the change
is future, but is certain and close at hand.

2, 3. Whilst the sunshine illuminates Jerusalem, the rest of
the world remains in darkness. The heathen peoples are accordingly drawn to the one centre of light on earth.

4. The coming of the Gentiles will satisfy Zion's desire for
the due appreciation of her spiritual preeminence ; but the longing
of her heart can only be satisfied by the restoration of her banished
children.

they all : the pronoun points forward to the end of the verse,
referring to the Jewish exiles, 'thy sons and daughters.'

carried...arms : lit. 'nursed upon the side,' i.e. on the hip,
the Eastern manner of carrying young children. For the thought,
cp. xlix. 22 ; lxvi. 12.

5-9. All the nations of the world will gather to Zion,
bringing over land and sea their choicest possessions as an
offering. By their tribute Zion and its Temple shall be
enriched and glorified.

5. tremble...enlarged : i.e. shall beat with joyful expectation, and experience relief from the restrictions and fears of
the past afflictions.

abundance of the sea : not the products of the ocean, but
rich cargoes from lands across the seas.

6. From the lands of the East and the South long trains of
camels, and flocks of sheep (*v.* 7), are to be seen wending their

thee, the dromedaries of Midian and Ephah ; they all shall
come from Sheba : they shall bring gold and frankincense,
7 and shall proclaim the praises of the LORD. All the flocks
of Kedar shall be gathered together unto thee, the rams
of Nebaioth shall minister unto thee : they shall come up
with acceptance on mine altar, and I will glorify the house
8 of my glory. Who are these that fly as a cloud, and as
9 the doves to their windows ? Surely the isles shall wait
for me, and the ships of Tarshish first, to bring thy
sons from far, their silver and their gold with them, for

---

way to Zion. With them are caravans conveying treasures of
gold and incense.

Midian : a nomadic people of the Sinaitic peninsula and the
deserts east of Palestine, cp. Gen. xxxvii. 28, 36 etc.

Ephah : a tribe closely related to Midian (Gen. xxv. 4).

they all : rather 'all they from Sheba shall come.' Sheba
was a district of S. Arabia, now known as Yemen, and specially
famous in ancient times for frankincense. It is to be distinguished from the Seba mentioned in xliii. 3.

7. Kedar...Nebaioth : important pastoral tribes of N. Arabia.
For Kedar, cp. xxi. 16; xlii. 11; Jer. xlix. 28. The Nebaioth
are in all probability to be identified with the Nabateans,
a people who attained considerable power in the last two
centuries B.C.

minister : by providing animals for the Temple sacrifices.

I will glorify...glory : or 'I will beautify...beauty.' The
phrase is ambiguous. It may imply that the Temple already
exists and requires only to be adorned. But, since the whole
scene lies in the ideal future, it may equally be taken to mean
that Yahwe will *then* have a temple which He will make
glorious.

8. The prophet once more turns to the Western world, and
sees the vision of a multitude ('cloud') of sailing ships, speeding
white-winged across the seas, like doves on their homeward way.

9. This fleet conveys the children of Jerusalem back from
their exilic homes ; and they return, not as poverty-stricken
outcasts, but as rich men bringing their wealth with them.

Surely...wait : the sense must be 'shall be watching in
readiness to observe and obey Yahwe's signal for the restoration
of Israel.' An alteration, affecting only one consonant of the
text, yields the much more suitable meaning 'Surely ships shall
be assembled for me....'

ships of Tarshish : large merchant vessels, cp. ii. 16.

the name of the LORD thy God, and for the Holy One
of Israel, because he hath glorified thee.

10–14. *The Gentiles shall build Jerusalem.*

And strangers shall build up thy walls, and their kings 10
shall minister unto thee : for in my wrath I smote thee,
but in my favour have I had mercy on thee.   Thy gates 11
also shall be open continually ; they shall not be shut day
nor night ; that men may bring unto thee the wealth of
the nations, and their kings led *with them.*   For that 12
nation and kingdom that will not serve thee shall perish ;
yea, those nations shall be utterly wasted.   The glory of 13
Lebanon shall come unto thee, the fir tree, the pine,
and the box tree together ; to beautify the place of my
sanctuary, and I will make the place of my feet glorious.

10–14.   Nor will the Jews themselves bear the labour of
rebuilding the desolate city ; for the Gentile nations will humbly
undertake this task, and beautify Zion with their gifts.

10.   thy walls : the walls of Jerusalem were not actually
rebuilt until the days of Nehemiah (*c.* 445 B.C.), who accomplished
their repair with the support of the Persian Government.   The
present verse anticipates that the heathen nations who destroyed
will also restore the city.

11.   But, although Zion be equipped with the means of
defence, these will not need to be used.   Peace will reign in the
land, and Zion's gates will require to be open day and night to
receive the endless stream of gifts.

led (with them) : the phrase suggests that the kings are
captive and brought by compulsion, but that is alien to the
context.   Perhaps therefore we should read, changing one
letter, 'their kings leading them.'

12.   The verse is unmetrical, disturbs the natural sequence
of *vv.* 11 and 13, is out of keeping with the sentiment of the
passage (see esp. *v.* 3) ; and may therefore with confidence be
deleted as a gloss.   For the thought, cp. Zech. xiv. 17, 18.

13.   glory of Lebanon : perhaps a term for the cedar, the
tree for which Mt Lebanon was famous ; or, generally, the
fine timber of the mountain.

fir...pine...box : or 'cypress...plane...sherbin-tree.' Cp. xli. 19.
place of my feet : i.e. 'the Temple,' for the phrase is
simply appositional to the preceding 'place of my sanctuary,'
cp. Ezek. xliii. 7.

14 And the sons of them that afflicted thee shall come
bending unto thee ; and all they that despised thee shall
bow themselves down at the soles of thy feet ; and
they shall call thee The city of the LORD, The Zion of
the Holy One of Israel.

15–18. *The transformation of Zion.*

15 Whereas thou hast been forsaken and hated, so that
no man passed through thee, I will make thee an
16 eternal excellency, a joy of many generations. Thou
shalt also suck the milk of the nations, and shalt suck
the breast of kings : and thou shalt know that I the
LORD am thy saviour, and thy redeemer, the Mighty One
17 of Jacob. For brass I will bring gold, and for iron I will
bring silver, and for wood brass, and for stones iron :
I will also make thy officers peace, and thine exactors
18 righteousness. Violence shall no more be heard in thy
land, desolation nor destruction within thy borders ; but
thou shalt call thy walls Salvation, and thy gates Praise.

15–18. How wonderful the transformation will be ! Zion
has experienced hatred and desolation (16ᵃ), has heard the
sounds of battle and destruction (*v.* 18ᵃ). Now she will enjoy
ceaseless admiration (*v.* 15ᵇ), wealth, wonderful adornment
(*vv.* 16, 17), and perfect security (*v.* 18ᵇ).

15. so that...through thee : travel, and therefore commerce,
ceased.

16. For 16ᵃ, cp. xlix. 23 ; and for 16ᵇ, xlix. 26.

17. For brass...iron: cp. 1 Kings x. 21, 27 ; and for the
opposite process, 1 Kings xiv. 26 f.

I will...righteousness : translate ' I will appoint Peace as
thy government and Righteousness as thy ruler.' In place of
the tyrannous control which foreign governors and garrisons
have exercised in the enfeebled city, there shall be established
a government of Peace and Righteousness. (For the personification of these ethical qualities, cp. lix. 14.)

18. thy walls...Praise : the walls are the sign of the city's
security, whilst the open gates, by reason of the throng of
strangers passing through them day and night, are symbolic of
the praise Yahwe will receive from mankind.

19-22.   *The Presence of Yahwe: Zion's joy.*

The sun shall be no more thy light by day ; neither 19
for brightness shall the moon give light unto thee :
but the LORD shall be unto thee an everlasting light, and
thy God thy glory.   Thy sun shall no more go down, 20
neither shall thy moon withdraw itself : for the LORD
shall be thine everlasting light, and the days of thy
mourning shall be ended.   Thy people also shall be all 21
righteous, they shall inherit the land for ever ; the branch
of my planting, the work of my hands, that I may be
glorified.   The little one shall become a thousand, and 22
the small one a strong nation : I the LORD will hasten
it in its time.

lxi.   *Good tidings proclaimed to Israel.*

1-3.   *The speaker declares his message.*

The spirit of the Lord GOD is upon me ; because the **61**

19-22.   Above all, Zion shall rejoice in the continual Presence
of Yahwe, and shall thereby dwell in eternal light.   Joy, holiness,
and power, are to be its everlasting possession.

19, 20.   Jerusalem shall no longer require the light of sun
and moon, for the continual Presence of Yahwe will cause an
unfailing and glorious light to shine in the midst of the city,
cp. Rev. xxi. 23.

21.   Never again shall Yahwe have to deprive a sinful Israel
of its land, for all the inhabitants of the new Zion shall be holy
in moral character.

branch : lit. 'a shoot,' sapling.

22.   little one : i.e. the smallest household.

thousand : or rather 'a clan,' a group of families.   The
community at present so small in numbers shall thus become a
great and powerful nation.

will...time : when the proper moment arrives Yahwe will
swiftly consummate this glorious transformation.

lxi. 1-3.   This chapter continues the theme of the glories of
the new era, but is addressed not to the capital but to the
nation.   In these opening verses the speaker announces that he
has received the call of Yahwe to proclaim to Israel a message
of comfort from its God, who promises the restoration of its

LORD hath anointed me to preach good tidings unto the meek ; he hath sent me to bind up the brokenhearted, to proclaim liberty to the captives, and the opening *of the* 2 *prison* to them that are bound ; to proclaim the acceptable year of the LORD, and the day of vengeance of 3 our God ; to comfort all that mourn ; to appoint unto them that mourn in Zion, to give unto them a garland for

---

exiles, and the renewal of joy and prosperity. In certain respects the language in which the speaker set forth his Divine call is reminiscent of the Servant-songs, and may easily have been influenced by them. But it is a mistake to suppose that the speaker is the ideal Servant. Any resemblances there may be (e.g. the endowment of the Spirit [xlii. 1], the comforting and emancipating ministry [l. 4, xlii. 7, xlix. 9]) are far outweighed by the differences. Here the speaker is not the mediator of the blessings but simply their herald, nor is he commissioned to the Gentiles (see *v.* 2) but only to the Jews. The herald is certainly an individual, and it is best to conclude that the prophet is speaking in reference to his own call.

1. The spirit…me : the speaker has received the essential endowment of the true herald, cp. xlii. 1 ; xlviii. 16. See the quotation in Luke iv. 18–21.

anointed : the word is meant metaphorically, 'hath consecrated me.'

the meek : here the word is used not of a humble-minded, submissive attitude, but rather of poverty or affliction : so marg. rightly 'the poor.' Similarly 'brokenhearted' means probably the crushed and downcast victims of persecution.

captives…bound…mourn : either of the actual return of the Jews of the Dispersion, or perhaps metaphorically, of spiritual captivity.

opening : the LXX has 'opening of the eyes of the blind.'

2. the acceptable…Lord : rather 'a year of Yahwe's favour,' cp. xlix. 8.

day of vengeance : i.e. on the peoples which have oppressed Israel, but perhaps the prophet has also in mind the wicked members of his nation. No comparison should be drawn between the *year* of favour and the *day* of vengeance ; both expressions are conventional. The revengeful attitude towards the Gentiles contrasts not only with the tone of lx. 3 but with II Isaiah's work in general, and tells against the view that this passage is by him.

3. a garland : lit. 'a festal turban.' This headdress, a sign of joy and prosperity, shall replace the ashes, which mourners

ashes, the oil of joy for mourning, the garment of praise
for the spirit of heaviness ; that they might be called
trees of righteousness, the planting of the LORD, that
he might be glorified.

4-11. *Description of the glorious future.*

And they shall build the old wastes, they shall raise up 4
the former desolations, and they shall repair the waste
cities, the desolations of many generations. And strangers 5
shall stand and feed your flocks, and aliens shall be your
plowmen and your vinedressers.   But ye shall be named 6
the priests of the LORD : men shall call you the ministers
of our God : ye shall eat the wealth of the nations, and in
their glory shall ye boast yourselves. For your shame 7

---

sprinkled on the head as a sign of their grief (lviii. 5; 2 Sam.
xiii. 19).

oil of joy: anointing with oil was performed as a token of
honour on festive occasions, cp. Ps. xlv. 7; Luke vii. 46.

garment of praise: i.e. renown, fame. The parallelism of
the verse is improved by reading 'oil of joy for the garment of
mourning, praise for....'

spirit of heaviness: lit. 'a failing (dimly burning) spirit,'
cp. xlii. 3.

trees: lit. 'oaks' or 'terebinths.'

the planting...glorified: cp. lx. 21.

4-9. The prophet now sets forth a picture of Israel's
prosperity in the coming age.

4. There shall be a restoration of the ancient buildings now
lying desolate and in ruins ; cp., for the same prediction, xlix. 8;
lviii. 12 ; lx. 10.

5, 6. Although in this ideal future the prophet conceives that
the Gentile nations will work for Israel's support (*v.* 5), the
relationship will not be that of slaves toiling for a master, but
rather of a community supporting a spiritual order in its
midst. In the new era, Israel shall be set apart for spiritual
service; it shall be the priest of the nations. Cp. lx. 10 and
Ex. xix. 6.

6. in their glory...yourselves: or, as marg., 'to their glory
ye shall succeed.' The precise meaning of the verb is uncertain.

7. The general sense of the verse is that the future felicity
will be so great as doubly to recompense Israel for all its past

ye shall have double ; and for confusion they shall rejoice
in their portion : therefore in their land they shall possess
8 double : everlasting joy shall be unto them.   For I the
LORD love judgement, I hate robbery with iniquity ; and
I will give them their recompence in truth, and I will
9 make an everlasting covenant with them.   And their seed
shall be known among the nations, and their offspring
among the peoples : all that see them shall acknowledge
them, that they are the seed which the LORD hath blessed.
10   I will greatly rejoice in the LORD, my soul shall be
joyful in my God ; for he hath clothed me with the
garments of salvation, he hath covered me with the robe
of righteousness, as a bridegroom decketh himself with
a garland, and as a bride adorneth herself with her jewels.
11 For as the earth bringeth forth her bud, and as the

---

suffering and shame.   The text, however, esp. in the first half
of the verse, is corrupt, and cannot be corrected with any
certainty.

8. Israel has been robbed and ill-treated by the heathen
nations, beyond its deserts, cp. Zech. i. 15. But God will
not permit this lawless increase of the punishment He had
to inflict upon His people. The Heb. (followed by A.V.)
has 'robbery with a burnt-offering,' which would make the
passage refer to the hypocritical conduct of certain Jews (cp.
ch. lviii.; Mal. iii. 8, 9), but the rendering is due to a misreading
of the Heb. consonants.

everlasting covenant : cp. lv. 3; lix. 21.

10.   I : is the speaker the prophet, or the redeemed community (or city)? The former is preferable, if the verse be an
integral part of this section ; but perhaps it may be said that
the prophet here expresses the feeling of the redeemed people
as a whole.   As, however, the verse is isolated, and breaks the
natural sequence of *vv.* 9, 11, it may be considered an addition.
Taken by itself, the verse is best regarded as an utterance of
Israel or Jerusalem.

salvation ‖ **righteousness** : synonyms for victory, deliverance.

decketh…garland : lit. performs priestly service with a festal
turban, cp. *v.* 3. The verb is inappropriate: read perhaps
'setteth up [on his head] a turban.'

11. The verse is connected with *v.* 9. For the thought of
the certainty that God will accomplish His promise, cp. lv. 10.

garden causeth the things that are sown in it to spring
forth ; so the Lord GOD will cause righteousness and
praise to spring forth before all the nations.

lxii.   *The Praises of Jerusalem, and the certainty of*
her approaching glory.

1-3.   *Zion's vindication is determined.*

For Zion's sake will I not hold my peace, and for **62**
Jerusalem's sake I will not rest, until her righteousness go
forth as brightness, and her salvation as a lamp that
burneth.   And the nations shall see thy righteousness, 2
and all kings thy glory : and thou shalt be called by
a new name, which the mouth of the LORD shall name.
Thou shalt also be a crown of beauty in the hand of 3
the LORD, and a royal diadem in the hand of thy God.

---

righteousness...praise : i.e. victory, and (consequently) praise.

lxii. 1-3. This chapter continues the theme of chs. lx., lxi. It
is marked, especially in the closing verses, by many reminiscences
of earlier passages. *vv.* 1-3 are sharply divided from *vv.* 4-12,
not indeed in subject, but by a change of metre. The first
three verses declare that the speaker will not rest until Zion's
redemption is come and its glory manifested to all the world.
Whether this speaker is God (who will not desist until His
purpose is achieved) or the prophet (who asserts that he will
not cease from his task—as declared in lxi. 1-3—until the Day
of Salvation arrives), is a matter on which opinions differ. In
favour of the view that it is the prophet who speaks is the fact
that the Lord is mentioned in the 3rd person in *vv.* 2, 3 : this,
however, is not decisive, for the same phenomenon is found in
lx. 19, 20, where God is assuredly the speaker. Moreover the
sentiment seems more appropriate, and certainly gains in force,
if it can be taken as the utterance of God Himself.

1. hold my peace...rest : i.e. refrain from judging and
punishing the wrongdoers—if God be the subject. If the
prophet, then the verse means that he will not cease to proclaim
his message.

lamp : better 'torch.'

2. the nations...glory : cp. lx. 2, 3.

a new name : the name in question is not that of *v.* 4, but a
mystery at present known only to God. It will be symbolic of
the new character of Zion and its redeemed position.

3. in the hand : evidently the prophet hesitates to describe

4, 5. The renewal of Zion's joy.

4 Thou shalt no more be termed Forsaken ; neither shall
thy land any more be termed Desolate : but thou shalt
be called Hephzi-bah, and thy land Beulah : for the LORD
5 delighteth in thee, and thy land shall be married.   For as
a young man marrieth a virgin, so shall thy sons marry
thee : and as the bridegroom rejoiceth over the bride, so
shall thy God rejoice over thee.

*6–9. The hope of Zion is ceaselessly remembered, and
rests on the guarantee of Yahwe's oath.*

6   I have set watchmen upon thy walls, O Jerusalem ;

Zion as a crown worn on the head of the Deity : he pictures it a
precious ornament resting in the Divine hand.

4–12.   As has been remarked, these verses are composed in a
different metre from that of *vv.* 1–3, but the theme is still the
future of Jerusalem in the coming glorious age. *vv.* 4, 5 picture
the transformation under the figures of a renaming of land and
city (*v.* 4), and a renewal of the marriage bliss which Jerusalem
had forfeited (*v.* 5).

4. Forsaken...Desolate : i.e. no longer deprived of the
Presence of Yahwe, her Husband, cp. xlix. 14 ; liv. 1, 6.

Hephzi-bah : lit. ' My delight is in her.'

Beulah : lit. ' married.'

5. thy sons : read ' thy Builder.'   The same change, a very
slight one in Heb., was required in xlix. 17.

6–9.   Day and night, without cessation, God hears from
Jerusalem the prayer for the accomplishment of His promise :
the promise which rests on the sure basis of His own word.
It is puzzling to determine who is the speaker in this passage.
That it is God is favoured by the first clause of *v.* 6, but
opposed (1) by the difficulty of supposing that He (*v.* 6b)
should have to command watchers (appointed by Himself) to
remind Him of His promise, and (2) by the use of ' the Lord '
(3rd pers.) in *vv.* 8, 9.   Although these objections are not
insuperable, it is easier to regard the prophet as the speaker.

6. I...watchmen : who are these watchers ? Probably angelic
beings, invisible guardians of the city, are intended.   It is, however, a strange statement that the prophet, presuming him to be
the speaker, should assert that *he* sets angelic watchers over the
city.   Either we must assume that this language, bold though

they shall never hold their peace day nor night : ye that
are the LORD'S remembrancers, take ye no rest, and give 7
him no rest, till he establish, and till he make Jerusalem
a praise in the earth. The LORD hath sworn by his 8
right hand, and by the arm of his strength, Surely I will
no more give thy corn to be meat for thine enemies ; and
strangers shall not drink thy wine, for the which thou
hast laboured : but they that have garnered it shall eat 9
it, and praise the LORD ; and they that have gathered it
shall drink it in the courts of my sanctuary.

10–12.　*Preparation must be made for the Return.*

Go through, go through the gates ; prepare ye the 10

---

it is, is possible in his prophetic fervour ; or else that *v.* 6ᵃ is
a quotation from some lost passage in which God is the speaker
(see, however, the previous note).　It is to be noted that
vv. 10–12 contain many echoes of earlier prophecies.

upon thy walls : better 'over thy walls,' which are still
unbuilt.

7.　The tone of the verse suggests a period when the expected
deliverance was felt to be strangely delayed.

8.　**no more** : in the future the people shall be enabled to
enjoy the full benefits of their labour, cp. lxv. 21, 22.　Evidently
it is implied that at present they are subjected to marauding
raids (perhaps of the Edomites, cp. Mal. i. 2–5), or the exactions
of foreign overlords.　The situation points to a post-exilic date.

9.　**the courts...sanctuary** : rather 'my holy courts.'　Since
the whole scene is laid in the ideal future, this phrase does not
necessarily imply the existence of the Temple.　Nevertheless it
obviously favours that inference, particularly when the previous
verse is taken into consideration.　It is further significant that
the plural 'courts' applies better to the second Temple (Neh.
xiii. 7) than to the first, which had only one court.　The
allusion is to the agricultural festivals held at the sanctuary
(Deut. xii. 17 f. etc.).

10–12.　All preparation must be made for the advent of the
citizens returning to Zion.　The Divine proclamation has gone
to the end of the earth, and Israel and its capital are finally
redeemed.　The passage is evidently based on xlviii. 20 ff.,
lii. 11, xl. 3, but the exact meaning is far from clear, see note
to *v.* 10.

10.　**Go...gates** : the command is uttered by the prophet, but

way of the people ; cast up, cast up the high way ; gather
11 out the stones ; lift up an ensign for the peoples.   Behold,
the LORD hath proclaimed unto the end of the earth,
Say ye to the daughter of Zion, Behold, thy salvation
cometh ; behold, his reward is with him, and his recom-
12 pence before him.   And they shall call them The holy
people, The redeemed of the LORD : and thou shalt be
called Sought out, A city not forsaken.

lxiii. 1–6.   *The return of the avenging God.*

63   Who is this that cometh from Edom, with dyed

---

to whom is it addressed ?   To the people of Jerusalem, who are
bidden to issue from its gates and prepare a triumphal highway
for the entry of the new inhabitants who are to throng into it?
Or are the gates those of Babylon (or any city which harbours
Jews of the Dispersion), the command being directed to exiled
Jews, bidding them prepare a road for return?   If the latter
view were adopted, it would not of course be necessary to infer
that the passage dates from before the fall of Babylon in 538 B.C.,
for it is quite certain that Jerusalem was in hopes of a further
return of Israelites from Babylon and elsewhere after the time
of Cyrus.   Either opinion is tenable, but the first is better suited
to the language.

prepare…people : great as is the general resemblance here to
xl. 3, the differences are still more striking.   In xl. 3 angelic
beings are to prepare a supernatural highway for Yahwe by
the removal of every natural obstacle, however vast.   Here the
command is given, apparently, to human beings, and the road is
conceived as a natural highway, to be prepared by the banking
up of earth and the removal of rough stones.   Possibly the
whole figure, as in lvii. 14, is intended to be understood metaphorically.

lift up…peoples : cp. xlix. 22, where, however, it is God
Himself who is said to lift up the standard.

11.   Cp. xlviii. 20 ('end of the earth'), and xl. 10, on which
passage the remainder of this verse is clearly modelled.

12.   The holy people : i.e. in virtue of their relationship to
the redeeming God, cp. lxi. 6; lxiii. 18.

Sought out : the name signifies the reversal of the state of
desolation referred to in lx. 15, lxii. 4 (cp. Jer. xxx. 17).   For a
similar alteration of titles, see Hos. i. 6–9, ii. 19–22; Jer. xx. 3.

lxiii. 1–6.   These wonderful verses have no immediate connection with the preceding group, cp. lx.–lxii., and are likewise

garments from Bozrah? this that is glorious in his
apparel, marching in the greatness of his strength?
I that speak in righteousness, mighty to save. Wherefore 2
art thou red in thine apparel, and thy garments like
him that treadeth in the winefat?   I have trodden the 3

---

independent of the sequel, lxiii. 7 ff. ; but they are akin in
feeling and, to some extent, in expression, with lix. 15ᵇ–20.
From Jerusalem a startled watchman (? the prophet) perceives
the majestic figure of a warrior God, advancing towards the
city. He asks the meaning of the blood-stained garments in
which the figure is clad, receiving answer, that it is Yahwe
Himself, returning from solitary combat in the land of Edom,
victorious, and crimsoned with the blood of His foes.

1. Who is this : the question is put by someone (either the
prophet himself, or simply an undefined spectator) who keeping
watch from Jerusalem descries the approach of the Divine
figure.

Edom...Bozrah : Bozrah : a city of Edom. The enmity
between Edom and the post-exilic community of Jerusalem was
peculiarly bitter. Dating from the venomous hostility shown
by Edom at the fall of Jerusalem (see Ezek. xxv. 12, xxxv. 5,
10 ff.; Obad. 10–16), the hatred seems to have been augmented
by frequent Edomite raids, cp. Mal. i. 2–5, and Is. xxxiv. 5–17
(a post-exilic passage). The conflict is fought in the land of
Edom, but from *vv.* 3, 6, it is clear that the Divine vengeance
is upon all nations which have incurred Yahwe's wrath. Edom,
however, is named as typical, or as the worst, of all such
peoples ; and there is no need, in view of the similar passage
xxxiv. 5–17, to eliminate the name by reading, as has been
suggested, 'Who is this that cometh reddened, with garments
more crimson than the grape-gatherer's.'

dyed : rather 'crimsoned,' i.e. blood-stained.

I...save : the majestic Warrior needs not to give His name,
but only to announce those unique attributes, which reveal Him
to be Yahwe, Israel's faithful ('I that speak in righteousness')
and redeeming ('mighty to save') God.

2. The questioner now seeks to know the reason of the
blood-stained robes.

red in : better 'wherefore is there red on....' There is in
Heb. a play of words between 'Edom' and 'red' (*'ădom*).

winefat : or 'winepress,' in the upper trough of which the
juice was trodden out of the grapes and allowed to flow thence
into the receptacle in the lower part of the press.

3. I have trodden : Yahwe replies, using the same figure of
speech, cp. Lam. i. 15 ; Rev. xix. 15.

winepress alone; and of the peoples there was no man
with me : yea, I trod them in mine anger, and trampled
them in my fury ; and their lifeblood is sprinkled upon
4 my garments, and I have stained all my raiment. For the
day of vengeance was in mine heart, and the year of my
5 redeemed is come. And I looked, and there was none to
help ; and I wondered that there was none to uphold :
therefore mine own arm brought salvation unto me ; and
6 my fury, it upheld me. And I trod down the peoples
in mine anger, and made them drunk in my fury, and
I poured out their lifeblood on the earth.

lxiii. 7–lxiv. 12. *A Prayer for the renewal of
Divine favour.*

lxiii. 7–14. *Yahwe's ancient mercies, and Israel's rebellion.*

7   I will make mention of the lovingkindnesses of the

    alone...with me : cp. lix. 16, and *v.* 5. The writer seems to
be living in a period, when Jerusalem has no prospect of
deliverance through a human champion.
    4. Compare lxi. 2. For 'year...redeemed,' translate rather
' year of my redemption,' i.e. the era of Divine favour.
    6. made them drunk : or 'and shattered them.'
    lxiii. 7–lxiv. 12. This section is in form a *prayer*, pathetically
earnest, that God will renew to His unhappy people the
mercies of ancient times. As such, it has no exact parallel in
Is. xl.–lxvi., and is certainly independent of the preceding and
succeeding section. A few phrases perhaps imply that the
Temple is in ruins and the land about Jerusalem devastated.
If the inference be correct, and if these verses are part of the
original text, two conclusions are possible : either the passage
was written before 518 B.C. (when the Temple was rebuilt),
or the reference is to some destruction of the Temple which
occurred at a much later date—see further the notes on lxiii. 18,
and lxiv. 10–12. If we cannot rely on these verses for guidance,
it must be owned that we have no satisfactory evidence as to the
date of the passage. The thoughts are applicable to any period
when Israel as a whole, or the godly members of the nation,
were in distress ; and as for the style, all that can be said is
that it lacks the distinctive traits of II Isaiah's writings, that
possibly but not certainly it might be from the same source as
chs. lvi.–lix., and that in some respects it resembles the style of
certain Psalms.

LORD, *and* the praises of the LORD, according to all that the LORD hath bestowed on us; and the great goodness toward the house of Israel, which he hath bestowed on them according to his mercies, and according to the multitude of his lovingkindnesses. For he said, Surely, they are my people, children that 8 will not deal falsely: so he was their saviour. In all 9 their affliction he was afflicted, and the angel of his presence saved them: in his love and in his pity he redeemed them; and he bare them, and carried them all the days of old. But they rebelled, and grieved his holy 10 spirit: therefore he was turned to be their enemy, *and* himself fought against them. Then he remembered the 11 days of old, Moses, *and* his people, *saying*, Where is he that brought them up out of the sea with the shepherds

---

7-14. The writer recalls the manifold instances of Yahwe's mercy to His people in the days of old (*vv.* 7-9), and then confessing the iniquity which has compelled the Divine anger (*v.* 10) he dwells again with wistful longing on the vanished days of grace (*vv.* 11-14).

7. praises: better 'praiseworthy acts.'

8, 9. so he was...them: rather, with LXX, 'so he was their saviour in all their affliction. Not a messenger nor an angel but his own Presence saved them.' The text, as it stands, 'in all their afflictions he was afflicted' presents a beautiful thought, but one which is without parallel in the O.T., the nearest approach to it being found in Jud. x. 16.

10. his holy spirit: not simply 'His divine spirit,' but an indwelling (*v.* 11) Presence of God Himself in the nation, affecting the people as a pure and sensitive moral principle, both guiding them ('causing them to rest,' *v.* 14) and being vexed by their perversity (cp. Eph. iv. 30; Acts vii. 51).

11. he remembered: the pronoun must refer to Israel, since the question 'Where is he..., etc.' is obviously put by the people or someone speaking in their name.

Moses...people: it is just possible that *v.* 11ᵃ should be rendered 'Then His people remembered the ancient days of Moses,' but more probably the words 'Moses' and 'his people' are glosses, the former anticipating 'shepherd' and the latter 'flock' (see below).

Where...flock: better, with LXX, 'Where is He that brought

of his flock? where is he that put his holy spirit in the
12 midst of them? that caused his glorious arm to go at the
right hand of Moses? that divided the water before them,
13 to make himself an everlasting name? that led them
through the depths, as an horse in the wilderness, that
14 they stumbled not? As the cattle that go down into the
valley, the spirit of the LORD caused them to rest: so
didst thou lead thy people, to make thyself a glorious
name.

15–19. *A cry for mercy.*

15 Look down from heaven, and behold from the habitation
of thy holiness and of thy glory: where is thy zeal and
thy mighty acts? the yearning of thy bowels and thy
16 compassions are restrained toward me. For thou art our
father, though Abraham knoweth us not, and Israel doth
not acknowledge us: thou, O LORD, art our father; our

---

up from the sea the shepherd of His flock,' i.e. delivered Moses
from the Red Sea. In any case the reference is to the rescue of
Israel from the Egyptians at the Red Sea. The plural 'shepherds'
of the Heb. text alludes of course to Moses and Aaron.

13. as...wilderness: safely and easily, as a horse might
travel over open prairie-land, so Israel passed through the bed
of the sea.

14. caused...rest: i.e. brought them to the fertile land of
Canaan, like cattle to a rich pasturage. The ancient versions
support a variant reading 'led them.'

15–19. Leaving the memories of the past, the speaker on
behalf of his brethren breaks into a passionate invocation of the
Divine pity. Oh, that Yahwe, remembering His abiding Fatherhood, would at last relieve His people!

15. The writer feels that God has not only withdrawn His
presence from Jerusalem to Heaven, but even there on high
has turned his eyes away from the doings of man on earth.
For the image, cp. Ps. xiv. 2.

are restrained...me: read either, as LXX, 'towards us,'
or—placing the mark of interrogation after 'compassions'—
'Restrain not thyself.'

16. our father: not individually (for the O.T. does not
attain to the height of that conception) but collectively. As the
founder of the nation by the act of its redemption from Egypt,
Yahwe is its Father, cp. lxiv. 8; Exod. iv. 22; Mal. ii. 10 etc.

redeemer from everlasting is thy name. O LORD, why 17
dost thou make us to err from thy ways, and hardenest
our heart from thy fear? Return for thy servants' sake,
the tribes of thine inheritance. Thy holy people possessed 18
it but a little while : our adversaries have trodden down
thy sanctuary.   We are become as they over whom thou 19
never barest rule ; as they that were not called by thy
name.

lxiv. 1–7. *An appeal that God will manifest Himself.*

Oh that thou wouldest rend the heavens, that thou **64**
wouldest come down, that the mountains might flow down

17. why...heart : a surprising statement, which seems to
imply that Yahwe, by His stern attitude, has deliberately increased Israel's sinfulness; cp. Exod. vii. 3, where God is
said to harden the heart of Pharaoh.   The O.T. writers are
agreed in regarding men as responsible for their actions : *moral*
evil is the result of personal human choice.   All such phrases
as that of the text must be interpreted, not as though the writer
would accuse God of augmenting moral evil in men, but as an
attempt to express the inevitable result of the law of moral
development, 'he that hath to him shall be given, and he that
hath not from him shall be taken away even that which he hath'
(Mark iv. 25) ; i.e. 'hardening of heart' is just the increasing
loss of spiritual capacity, which inevitably accompanies sin and
is its nemesis.
   from thy fear : rather 'so that we fear thee not.'
   18. Thy holy...while : the statement that Israel possessed
it (*sc.* the Temple) 'but a little while' presents an insoluble
problem.   Manifestly the phrase is inapplicable to Solomon's
Temple, which stood until the sack of Jerusalem in 587 B.C. ;
and there is no evidence for the theory that the second Temple
(dedicated in 516 B.C.) was destroyed shortly afterwards.   Had
such a disaster occurred, it would surely have been alluded to
in the records of Ezra or Nehemiah.   Nor is the guess that the
Temple may have been destroyed in the time of Artaxerxes
Ochus (385–337) supported by any reliable evidence.   There is
therefore good reason to accept the emendation 'Wherefore
do the wicked despise (or 'march over') thy holy place.'   The
correction required is very simple in Heb.
   our...sanctuary : see note on lxiv. 11.
   lxiv. 1–7. The prayer breaks into a cry of uttermost longing,
that God would manifest Himself from the silent Heavens, and,

2 at thy presence ; as when fire kindleth the brushwood,
and the fire causeth the waters to boil : to make thy name
known to thine adversaries, that the nations may tremble
3 at thy presence !   When thou didst terrible things which
we looked not for, thou camest down, the mountains
4 flowed down at thy presence.   For from of old men have
not heard, nor perceived by the ear, neither hath the
eye seen a God beside thee, which worketh for him that
5 waiteth for him.   Thou meetest him that rejoiceth and
worketh righteousness, those that remember thee in thy
ways : behold, thou wast wroth, and we sinned : in them
6 *have we been* of long time, and shall we be saved?   For
we are all become as one that is unclean, and all our
righteousnesses are as a polluted garment : and we all

---

to the terror of His foes, would display His moral majesty and
power.   The text, especially in *vv.* 4–7, has suffered serious
disturbance.

   1.   Cp. lxvi. 15.   For the images of the desired theophany,
cp. Jud. v. 4, 5 ; Ps. xviii. 7–9 ; Hab. iii. 3–6 ; Mic. i. 4.

   flow : better, as marg., 'quake.'

   2.   As neither wood nor water are able to resist the action of
fire upon them, so Yahwe is entreated to appear in resistless
might.

   3.   **When...didst** : connect the clause with the previous verse :
'...thy presence, whilst thou doest terrible things.'

   thou camest...presence : to be deleted, as an accidental
repetition from *v.* 1.

   4.   The first clause is better if read in conjunction with *v.* 3ª,
'...looked not for, and of which from of old men have not
heard.'   Then, commencing a fresh sentence, 'Ear hath not
perceived, nor eye seen....'   A few slight changes are required
for this rendering, but the text as it stands is certainly confused.

   5.   **Thou meetest** : read 'Oh, that thou wouldest meet him
that joyfully worketh righteousness.'

   and we sinned : apparently 'sinned still deeper in consequence
of the Divine anger,' but see note to lxiii. 17.

   in them...saved : the text is undoubtedly corrupt, and the
emendations proposed are very uncertain.

   6, 7.   A mournful acknowledgement of the national degeneracy
and of its consequence, the cessation of the Divine recognition.

do fade as a leaf ; and our iniquities, like the wind, take us away.   And there is none that calleth upon thy name, 7 that stirreth up himself to take hold of thee : for thou hast hid thy face from us, and hast consumed us by means of our iniquities.

8–12. *An appeal for help to the Father-God.*

But now, O LORD, thou art our father ; we are the clay, 8 and thou our potter ; and we all are the work of thy hand. Be not wroth very sore, O LORD, neither remember 9 iniquity for ever : behold, look, we beseech thee, we are all thy people.   Thy holy cities are become a wilderness, 10 Zion is become a wilderness, Jerusalem a desolation. Our 11 holy and our beautiful house, where our fathers praised

---

6.   Even at the highest estimate the nation remains 'unclean,' i.e. ceremonially impure, and so unable to draw near to God.

iniquities...wind : the national sinfulness, through the disasters it has brought upon the community, sweeps away the individual Jews in great numbers, like the falling leaves of a tree in autumn.

7. hast consumed us : lit. 'hast melted us.'   But the LXX gives a preferable reading 'hast delivered us into the hand (power) of our iniquities.'

8–12.   The prayer concludes with a piteous supplication to God, imploring Him, despite Israel's failure, to remember His unchanging Fatherhood (*vv.* 8–10).   The land is ravaged, Jerusalem desolate, the Temple burnt with fire !   Surely Yahwe at last will show mercy (*vv.* 10–12).

8. we are...potter : perverse as the nation (the clay) may have been, if God (the potter) will have patience, He can still mould their destiny with resistless power.   For this famous simile, cp. xlv. 9 ; Jer. xviii. 4–6 ; Job x. 9.

10.   **Thy holy cities** : the townships of Judah, the 'holy land' (Zech. ii. 12).

11.   **Our holy place...fire** : the present verse and the last clause of lxiii. 18 speak of the Temple as a ruin, destroyed by fire. This would seem to make it certain that the passage must be dated before the rebuilding of the Temple in 518 B.C., and, in the state of our present information, this is the safest view. Some scholars, however, consider that the reference may be to a

thee, is burned with fire ; and all our pleasant things are
12 laid waste.   Wilt thou refrain thyself for these things, O
LORD ; wilt thou hold thy peace, and afflict us very sore?

lxv., lxvi.   *The reward of the faithful and the doom of
the wicked.*

lxv. 1–7.   *The gross superstitions of certain hardened apostates.*

65   I am inquired of by them that asked not *for me* ;
I am found of them that sought me not : I said, Behold
me, behold me, unto a nation that was not called by

destruction of the Temple in the time of Artaxerxes Ochus,
358–337 B.C. (the tradition, however, is not attested by any
conclusive evidence), or even to the burning of the Temple
which certainly took place in the reign of Antiochus Epiphanes,
king of the Seleucid Empire.   The latter theory, though suitable
as to the fact, involves a very late date, unlikely for the passage
as a whole, but less difficult, if (as some suppose) the present
verse and lxiii. 18 are glosses.

pleasant things : i.e. the treasures and ornaments of Temple
and city, Lam. i. 10.

12. for these things : i.e. despite these disasters.

lxv., lxvi.   Although frequent changes of metre suggest the
likelihood that these two chapters were not originally composed
as a continuous discourse, almost all the verses deal with the
contrast between the fate of the saints and that in store for the
party of cruel and heathenish apostates.   Both chapters imply
the existence of the Temple and, in general, conditions analogous
to those of lvi. 9–lvii. 21.   The outstanding feature is the im-
passable gulf (lxvi. 5) which severs the servants of God from
their degenerate persecutors who are past repentance.   The
prophet looks only for the annihilation of those apostates,
and for the blissful vindication of the righteous remnant.   The
most probable date would therefore seem to be *c.* 500–450 B.C.,
the gloomy period preceding the advent of Ezra and Nehemiah.

lxv. 1–7.   There are those who have scorned the efforts of
Yahwe to win them to the true faith, and have abandoned themselves to loathsome forms of superstition : *their* doom is at hand.

1. I am inquired...me not : render 'I let myself be inquired
of by those that asked not ; I let myself be found by those that
sought me not,' i.e. the indifference of the sinners is set in contrast to the active solicitude of Yahwe who has shown Himself
eager to save them from their ways.

that was...name : read 'that did not call upon my name.'

my name.   I have spread out my hands all the day unto 2
a rebellious people, which walketh in a way that is not
good, after their own thoughts ;   a people that provoketh 3
me to my face continually, sacrificing in gardens, and
burning incense upon bricks ; which sit among the graves, 4
and lodge in the secret places ;   which eat swine's flesh,

1, 2.   In Rom. x. 20, 21, St Paul treats *v.* 1 as relating to the
conversion of the Gentiles, and *v.* 2 to the faithlessness of Israel.
Though the language lends itself to that interpretation, it is
certain that the writer intended to refer to the same persons
throughout.

3.   a people : i.e. (as elsewhere in the chapter) Israel, or
strictly speaking, the degenerate portion of the nation.   So
gross (*vv.* 3^b-5) are the heathen rites committed by these persons
who regard themselves as Israelites that there is not a little likelihood in the suggestion that the apostates denounced here and
in the following chapters are primarily those half-caste Jews, the
Samaritans, who claimed to be worshippers of Yahwe but in
reality were steeped in the customs of their heathen ancestors.
But it may well be that their practices were aided and abetted
by many debased members of the Jerusalem community, for it
is probable that a large number of the poor Jews, left behind in
Judaea at the time of the captivity, had sunk into paganism.
The famous feud between the Samaritans and the orthodox Jews
of Jerusalem dates (according to Ezra iv. 1-3) from the refusal
of Zerubbabel (*c.* 537 B.C.) to allow the former to participate in
restoring the Temple.

gardens : see note to lxvi. 17, and cp. i. 29.

upon bricks : or ' upon the tiles.'   No certain explanation
of the phrase has yet been given.   Perhaps the ' tiles ' are those
of the roofs, in which case the allusion may be to the worship of
star-gods (2 Kings xxi. 3, 5) by burning incense on the flat
housetops.   Another conjectural translation is 'beside the white
poplars,' a tree associated with the deities of the underworld.

4.   sit...secret places : in hope of obtaining oracles from
the dead, cp. viii. 19.   For 'lodge' translate 'pass the night.'
The 'secret-places' are recesses of caves used for necromantic
rites.

swine's flesh : the point here is not so much that the Jewish
law forbade the eating of pork (Lev. xi. 7 ; 2 Macc. vi. 18), but
rather the fact on which that prohibition was based ; namely,
that the pig was sacred to various heathen deities, and in the
present case was being eaten in their honour.

5 and broth of abominable things is in their vessels ; which
say, Stand by thyself, come not near to me, for I am
holier than thou : these are a smoke in my nose, a fire
6 that burneth all the day.   Behold, it is written before me :
I will not keep silence, but will recompense, yea, I will
7 recompense into their bosom, your own iniquities, and
the iniquities of your fathers together, saith the LORD,
which have burned incense upon the mountains, and
blasphemed me upon the hills : therefore will I first
measure their work into their bosom.

8–25.   The final state of the faithful and the faithless.

8   Thus saith the LORD, As the new wine is found in the
cluster, and one saith, Destroy it not, for a blessing is

---

abominable things : i.e. unclean animals, consecrated to
foreign gods ; cp. lxvi. 17.
5. for I am...thou : better 'lest I render thee sacrosanct
(taboo).' 'Sacredness' was considered to be contagious. The
clause is therefore a warning from the devotee that any who
touches him in his consecrated condition will be made 'holy'
and inhibited for the time being from secular affairs.
smoke...nose : either, those evil actions are a continual ('a
fire...all the day') source of irritation to God, stirring up his
anger ; or, these things are *a cause of* My anger (symbolised,
as in Ps. xviii. 8, by smoke proceeding from the nostrils).
6. yea...bosom : 'bosom,' i.e. the loose fold of the Eastern
costume. The clause has perhaps been transferred wrongly
from the end of *v.* 7, which would then read ' ...their work and
then requite it into their bosom.'
8–25. These verses portray the contrast between the fate of
the just servants of God and that of the faithless idolaters, when
Yahwe intervenes, as He assuredly will, to right the evil conditions which now exist. *vv.* 13–20 are in a different metre
from the rest of the section, and may be regarded as an independent poem.
8. As the...cluster : Israel resembles a cluster of grapes,
preserved only for the sake of its juice, which is to become the
fresh season's wine. Were it not for valuable juice (the faithful
minority) the bunch would be cast aside.
Destroy...in it : possibly the first line of a vintage song.
The 'blessing' is of course the wine-juice.

in it : so will I do for my servants' sakes, that I may not
destroy them all.   And I will bring forth a seed out of 9
Jacob, and out of Judah an inheritor of my mountains :
and my chosen shall inherit it, and my servants shall
dwell there.   And Sharon shall be a fold of flocks, and 10
the valley of Achor a place for herds to lie down in,
for my people that have sought me.   But ye that forsake 11
the LORD, that forget my holy mountain, that prepare
a table for Fortune, and that fill up mingled wine unto
Destiny ; I will destine you to the sword, and ye shall all 12
bow down to the slaughter : because when I called, ye
did not answer ; when I spake, ye did not hear ; but

---

9. A renewal of the great doctrine of 1 Isaiah, that God
would work out His purpose by preserving the few faithful
members of the community to be the recipients of His blessings.

10. Sharon : a luxuriant part of the maritime plain, lying
between Carmel and Joppa.   Achor, probably a valley leading
down to the Jordan near Jericho.   The two places are intended
to indicate that Israel's territory shall extend as far to West and
East as patriotic expectation could desire.

for my...me : the clause destroys the metre and may be
regarded as a gloss.

11, 12. Let the wicked idolaters contrast the fate to which
they are now destined.

11. my holy mountain : i.e. the Temple on Mount Zion,
cf. *v.* 25.

prepare...Destiny : the allusion in this extremely interesting
verse is to the pagan practice of spreading a table with wine and
viands as an offering for the gods.   The custom of preparing
these sacrificial banquets, known as *lectisternia*, was widely
observed among the ancients, the offering of the 'shew-bread'
(Ex. xxv. 30) being an unconscious survival in the ritual of
Jewish worship.   As for the gods mentioned here, 'Gad'
(translated 'Fortune' in the text) was an ancient Canaanite deity
of 'good-fortune,' widely worshipped in Syria and Palestine.
Of the other 'Meni' (Destiny) less is known.   Possibly the
name also signifies 'fortune' (or perhaps '*bad*-luck'); and it
may be the case that both deities were regarded as star-gods
presiding over human destinies.

destine : note the word-play with the name 'Destiny' above
(Heb. 'Meni...manah').

ye did that which was evil in mine eyes, and chose that
wherein I delighted not.

13   Therefore thus saith the Lord GOD, Behold my servants
shall eat, but ye shall be hungry : behold, my servants
shall drink, but ye shall be thirsty : behold, my servants
14 shall rejoice, but ye shall be ashamed : behold, my
servants shall sing for joy of heart, but ye shall cry
for sorrow of heart, and shall howl for vexation of spirit.
15 And ye shall leave your name for a curse unto my chosen,
and the Lord GOD shall slay thee ; and he shall call
16 his servants by another name : so that he who blesseth
himself in the earth shall bless himself in the God of
truth ; and he that sweareth in the earth shall swear
by the God of truth ; because the former troubles are
17 forgotten, and because they are hid from mine eyes.   For,
behold, I create new heavens and a new earth : and the
former things shall not be remembered, nor come into
18 mind.   But be ye glad and rejoice for ever in that which

13–20. The awful fate of the wicked is set in close comparison with the felicity which will be the reward of Yahwe's
servants.

15. for a curse : to call down on anyone such a fate as
theirs will be regarded as a dreadful curse.

by another name : not that the appellation 'Israel' will
cease.   The writer means that in the coming age the righteous,
who are now the objects of mockery and scorn, will be revered
as is fitting, and addressed by honourable titles.

16. in the earth : rather ' in the land.'   For the invocation
of a blessing in a revered name, cp. Gen. xii. 3, xxvi. 4, xlviii. 20.

former troubles : i.e. the persecutions of the godly in the
actual present and past time.

17–20. The poem advances to a glorious conclusion : the
pain and perils of the present life are all forgotten, and the
prophet rises to the vision of a new Heaven and a new earth, in
which God and man will alike rejoice.

17. create...earth : according to Hebrew thought the moral
condition of the human race affected its physical environment.
Thus, as when man falls into sin, the ground is cursed on his
account (Gen. iii. 17) ; so when he is saved, the universe will be
transformed (cp. xi. 6–9 ; xxxv. ; Joel iii. 18).

I create : for, behold, I create Jerusalem a rejoicing, and
her people a joy.   And I will rejoice in Jerusalem, and 19
joy in my people : and the voice of weeping shall be
no more heard in her, nor the voice .of crying.   There 20
shall be no more thence an infant of days, nor an old man
that hath not filled his days : for the child shall die
an hundred years old, and the sinner being an hundred
years old shall be accursed.   And they shall build houses, 21
and inhabit them ; and they shall plant vineyards, and
eat the fruit of them.   They shall not build, and another 22
inhabit ; they shall not plant, and another eat : for as the
days of a tree shall be the days of my people, and my
chosen shall long enjoy the work of their hands.   They 23
shall not labour in vain, nor bring forth for calamity ; for

---

18. a rejoicing : i.e. a cause for rejoicing, lx. 15.
20. Cp. Zech. viii. 4.   The period of human life shall be
marvellously prolonged, so that even those whose life is shortest
shall depart 'in a good old age.'
infant...his days : there shall be no cases of children dying
after the briefest spell of life, nor of men upon whom old age
comes prematurely.   'Infant of days' might be translated 'child
of one year old.'
the sinner...accursed : rather 'he that falls short of a
hundred years shall be accursed.'   Death even at that great
age will be reckoned so premature as to be the sign of having
incurred the Divine anger.
21-25. The theme of Israel's felicity in the new era is continued in these verses, but in the metre of *vv.* 8-12, which (as
has been said) differs from that of *vv.* 13-20.   The change may
be accounted for in several ways.   It may be that *vv.* 21-25 are
a later addition, an amplification of the chapter by some writer
who disregarded the metre of the poem, *vv.* 13-20, but had
worthily appreciated its thought.   Or we may hold that *vv.* 13-20
are an earlier poem incorporated by the writer of *vv.* 8-12 and
21-25 as a fitting expression of his own hopes.   Finally it is
possible that the chapter is by one writer, who was indifferent to
metrical unity, and purposely varied the poetical form of his
thought.
22. as...tree : sudden death will not occur to rob them of
the fruits of their labours.   Cp. lxii. 8, 9, where it is implied
that they will be immune from hostile raids.

they are the seed of the blessed of the LORD, and their
24 offspring with them.   And it shall come to pass that,
before they call, I will answer ; and while they are yet
25 speaking, I will hear.   The wolf and the lamb shall feed
together, and the lion shall eat straw like the ox : and
dust shall be the serpent's meat.   They shall not hurt nor
destroy in all my holy mountain, saith the LORD.

lxvi.   *The verdict of God against those who offer immoral
and degraded worship, compared with the eternal bliss which
awaits His righteous servants in the new and glorious
Jerusalem.*

66   Thus saith the LORD, The heaven is my throne, and
the earth is my footstool : what manner of house will
ye build unto me ? and what place shall be my rest ?

---

23. offspring with them : i.e., as marg., 'shall remain with
them.'
   25.   A quotation, with some variations, from xi. 6–9.
   dust...meat : an allusion to Gen. iii. 14.
   lxvi.   The final doom of the wicked and the glory of the
righteous, as in the previous chapter, are the leading subjects,
but so closely and so strangely are they interwoven that it is
very difficult to divide this chapter into any clearly-defined
sections.   In *v.* 6 the existence of the Temple is assumed, and
the general tone (except in the last two verses) makes it most
probable that the date is much the same as that of the preceding chapter.
   1–4.   A solemn warning to those who think to honour Yahwe
by the erection of a Temple, whilst worshipping Him with a
degraded and pagan ritual.   In view of other indications that
the Samaritans and their supporters are the apostate party
denounced in chs. lxv., lxvi., it is plausible to think that the
allusion in this verse is to the Samaritan project of building a
Temple to Yahwe on Mt Gerizim as a rival to that in Jerusalem,
a project which was eventually accomplished (in 433 or 333 B.C.)
—cp. John iv. 20.   It has been suggested that the passage is
earlier than 518 B.C. and is directed against the proposal to
rebuild the Temple in Jerusalem at that time ; but the allusion
to the Temple in *v.* 6 makes this view improbable.
   1. what...house...what place : i.e. (if the reference be to a
rival Temple) what house other than the Temple on Mt Zion ?

For all these things hath mine hand made, and *so* all 2
these things came to be, saith the LORD : but to this man
will I look, even to him that is poor and of a contrite
spirit, and that trembleth at my word.   He that killeth an 3
ox is as he that slayeth a man ; he that sacrificeth a
lamb, as he that breaketh a dog's neck ; he that offereth
an oblation, *as he that offereth* swine's blood ; he that
burneth frankincense, as he that blesseth an idol : yea,
they have chosen their own ways, and their soul delighteth
in their abominations ; I also will choose their delusions, 4
and will bring their fears upon them ; because when
I called, none did answer ; when I spake, they did not
hear : but they did that which was evil in mine eyes,
and chose that wherein I delighted not.

Hear the word of the LORD, ye that tremble at his 5

---

2.   came to be : read, with LXX, 'are mine.'
to this man : cp. lvii. 15.

3.   *as he that offereth* : the words are supplied by the trans-
lators, but give a legitimate interpretation to this difficult
sentence. Equally good, however, would be the rendering 'he
that...*doth also...*'; i.e. there are those who think they may
combine legitimate acts of worship with the evil practices
employed in pagan ritual (*v.* 3)—upon all such Yahwe will
bring fitting retribution (*v.* 4).

slayeth a man : i.e. human sacrifice, probably of children
(cp. lvii. 5).

dog's neck : Justin xviii. 1. 10 refers to the Carthaginians as
'sacrificing human beings, and eating the flesh of dogs' (i.e. sacramentally).

swine's blood : cp. *v.* 17 and lxv. 4.

4.   delusions : or 'mockings' or perhaps 'fretting.' The
meaning is clear : as the apostates chose their idolatries, so
God will 'choose' (i.e. approve) their distressful fate.

5-22.   Of these verses, *vv.* 5, 6, 15, 16, 18, 19 deal with the
calamities impending over the enemies of God, whilst *vv.* 7-14,
20-22 promise the advent of joy for the righteous, the repopulation of Jerusalem, and its complete felicity in the coming era of
Divine favour.

5, 6. · The mockery with which the apostates have taunted
the faithful Jews will recoil on themselves in a terrible retributive
judgement.

E.   9

word : Your brethren that hate you, that cast you out for
my name's sake, have said, Let the LORD be glorified,
that we may see your joy ; but they shall be ashamed.
6 A voice of tumult from the city, a voice from the temple,
a voice of the LORD that rendereth recompence to his
7 enemies. Before she travailed, she brought forth ; before
8 her pain came, she was delivered of a man child. Who
hath heard such a thing ? who hath seen such things ?
Shall a land be born in one day ? shall a nation be brought
forth at once ? for as soon as Zion travailed, she brought
9 forth her children. Shall I bring to the birth, and not
cause to bring forth ? saith the LORD : shall I that cause
to bring forth shut *the womb* ? saith thy God.

10   Rejoice ye with Jerusalem, and be glad for her, all ye
that love her : rejoice for joy with her, all ye that mourn
11 over her : that ye may suck and be satisfied with the
breasts of her consolations ; that ye may milk out, and
12 be delighted with the abundance of her glory. For thus
saith the LORD, Behold, I will extend peace to her like a
river, and the glory of the nations like an overflowing
stream, and ye shall suck *thereof* ; ye shall be borne upon

---

5. brethren : clearly the apostate party can claim kinship
with the true Jews, i.e. they are either Samaritans or paganised
descendants of the Jews left behind at the time of the captivity.

Let…joy : better 'Let Yahwe show Himself glorious, that'
etc. They taunt the righteous with their unrealised hopes.

they : i.e. the wicked. After all it is they, and not the
righteous, who have miscalculated the future.

6. The scene of fiery judgements, which is here pictured, is
continued at *v.* 15.

A voice : read, in each instance, 'Hark, a roar….'

7-14. The repopulation of Zion (*vv.* 7-9), the peace and
the glory with which God will make it joyful (*vv.* 10-14).

7. Before she travailed : the restoration of the people will
be miraculously swift.

12. glory of the nations : i.e. their riches and prosperity,
cp. lx. 5, 17 ; lxi. 6 ; and for the metaphor of the river,
cp. xlviii. 18.

the side, and shall be dandled upon the knees. As 13
one whom his mother comforteth, so will I comfort you;
and ye shall be comforted in Jerusalem. And ye shall 14
see *it*, and your heart shall rejoice, and your bones shall
flourish like the tender grass : and the hand of the LORD
shall be known toward his servants, and he will have
indignation against his enemies. For, behold, the LORD 15
will come with fire, and his chariots shall be like the
whirlwind ; to render his anger with fury, and his rebuke
with flames of fire. For by fire will the LORD plead, and 16
by his sword, with all flesh : and the slain of the LORD
shall be many. They that sanctify themselves and purify 17
themselves *to go* unto the gardens, behind one in the
midst, eating swine's flesh, and the abomination, and the
mouse ; they shall come to an end together, saith the

---

upon the side : see note to lx. 4. The Gentiles will foster
the life of the young community.

14. bones...grass : i.e. their physical frames shall be fresh
and vigorous.

15-19. The theme of God's judgement on the wicked,
which was introduced in *v.* 6, is here resumed and continues to
v. 19. That *v.* 17 refers to the practices of the apostate Jews
is clearly indicated by the close resemblance between it and *v.* 3.
Probably the writer feels that the judgement will begin with these
evil persons, but the language of *vv.* 16, 18, 19 plainly declares
that it will have a universal effect ('upon all flesh,' *v.* 16).

15. Cp. lxiv. 1. For the images of the theophany cp.
xxx. 27 ff.; Ps. xviii. 8 ff., lxviii. 17.

16. plead : i.e. enter into judgement.

17. unto the gardens : i.e. where the foul rites were celebrated,
cp. lxv. 3. It is natural that the places where springs and rivers
afford the blessing of luxuriant vegetation and cool shades
should ever have been the centres of worship in the hot lands of
the East.

behind...midst : a phrase of quite uncertain meaning. The
most plausible rendering of the existing text is 'after one in the
midst,' i.e. following the actions of some leader of the ceremonies.

abomination : a generic name for animals unclean in Jewish law.

mouse : forbidden in Lev. xi. 29. Like the dog and the
swine it was doubtless eaten sacramentally in the worship of
some heathen deity.

18 LORD. For I *know* their works and their thoughts : *the
time cometh, that I will gather all nations and tongues ;
19 and they shall come, and shall see my glory. And I will
set a sign among them, and I will send such as escape of
them unto the nations, to Tarshish, Pul and Lud, that
draw the bow, to Tubal and Javan, to the isles afar off,
that have not heard my fame, neither have seen my glory ;
20 and they shall declare my glory among the nations. And
they shall bring all your brethren out of all the nations
for an offering unto the LORD, upon horses, and in chariots,
and in litters, and upon mules, and upon swift beasts, to
my holy mountain Jerusalem, saith the LORD, as the

---

18. The text as it stands is untranslateable. An excellent
suggestion, involving only a small change in Hebrew, gives the
following translation for the last clause of *v.* 17 and the beginning of *v.* 18: 'their works and their thoughts together shall
come to an end, saith the Lord. And I am coming to gather....'

19. a sign : some startling act of retributive justice. So the
plagues of Egypt are termed 'signs' (Exod. vii. 3 etc.).

unto the nations : Yahwe will permit a certain number to
survive the great judgement, to the end that they may relate the
story to distant peoples who lie outside the circle of Israel's
immediate oppressors.

Tarshish...Javan : the names are drawn from the Book of
Ezekiel. By Tarshish is meant Tartessus, a port in Spain with
which Phoenician ships traded (ii. 16). For Pul read Put ; Put
and Lud were probably African nations. For 'that draw the
bow' read perhaps ' Meshech and Rosh,' the former a people of
Armenia. Tubal denotes the Tibareni of Pontus, whilst Javan
is certainly Ionia (the Greeks).

20–22. Recognising the relative innocence of these distant
peoples, the writer evidently considers they will not be included
in the catastrophe, provided they accept the warning of the
'sign' of God's glory and (*vv.* 20–22) carry out His purpose
by restoring to Jerusalem with all speed any of the Jews who
may be resident in their midst, cp. xliii. 6 ; xlix. 22 ; lx. 4, 9.
It is interesting to contrast the attitude of Ezekiel, who anticipated that even the outlying Gentiles (the hosts of Gog, Ezek.
xxxviii. f.) would display hostility to Israel and be overthrown
by Yahwe.

20. swift beasts : rather 'dromedaries.'

children of Israel bring their offering in a clean vessel
into the house of the LORD.   And of them also will I 21
take for priests *and* for Levites, saith the LORD.   For as 22
the new heavens and the new earth, which I will make,
shall remain before me, saith the LORD, so shall your
seed and your name remain.   And it shall come to pass, 23
that from one new moon to another, and from one sabbath
to another, shall all flesh come to worship before me,
saith the LORD.   And they shall go forth, and look upon 24
the carcases of the men that have transgressed against

---

as the children...Lord: i.e. with scrupulous and reverent
care.

21. of them also: i.e. of the Jews of the Dispersion, *not* of
the Gentiles whose function is simply to restore the exiles.

for priests (and) for Levites: lit. 'for priests, for Levites.'
Does this mean 'the priests, i.e. the Levites,' or (as the R.V.,
following the ancient versions, interprets) 'the priests as well
as the Levites'? If the latter, then the verse must be later than
the time of Ezra, when the legislation known as the Priestly
Code was introduced and established a distinction between the
Priests and the Levites as *classes*. Since the previous verses are
generally dated earlier than that period, this verse must be either
regarded as a later addition, or a single letter must be omitted
from the Hebrew, so as to give the translation 'for priests,
Levites.'

22. In conclusion Israel is assured that the blessings which
man and nature will enjoy in the new era are to be permanent.

23, 24. These two verses with much reason are considered
to be an appendix. Several details in the language, and
specially the sentiment expressed in *v.* 24, point to a late date.

23. from one...another: i.e. monthly, on the day of the new
moon ; and weekly, on the Sabbath.

all flesh: if the verse were by the author of the preceding
passages, the phrase would doubtless denote 'all nations of the
world, which have survived the judgement'—as it does in *v.* 16.
If, however, *vv.* 23, 24 are an appendix, it is much more
probable that the phrase refers simply to the Jews and such
proselytes as dwell in their midst ; and in that case the antithesis
'the men that have transgressed against me' (*v.* 24) will refer
specially to the godless apostate section of Israel.

24. The carcases of the rebels will lie exposed as a spectacle
to the righteous in one of the valleys outside the walls of
Jerusalem, there to be tormented eternally by the gnawing of

me : for their worm shall not die, neither shall their fire
be quenched ; and they shall be an abhorring unto all
flesh.

---

worms and the heat of fire. The exact locality in the writer's
mind may have been the valley of the Kidron, east of the city,
but in later times it was thought to be the valley of Hinnom
(*Greek* 'Gehenna') south of Jerusalem. Human sacrifices had
once been offered to Molech (Jer. vii. 31 f.) in this valley, which
was accordingly desecrated by King Josiah (2 Kings xxiii. 10)
and used as the place where was deposited all the refuse of the
city, including (so tradition relates) the corpses of criminals.
The imagery of this verse became popular in the later Jewish
conception of the torments awaiting the wicked after death, and
the name of the valley, Gehenna, was used to denote the place of
eternal punishment (cp. Mk. ix. 43 ; Luke xvi. 23).

    an abhorring : a late word, used elsewhere in the O.T. only in
Dan. xii. 2.

INDEX